Tales of the
Old Railwaymen

07

MY 2007

07

Tales of the
Old Railwaymen

Tom Quinn

David & Charles

*Thanks to all those railwaymen who agreed to be interviewed and
to Sue Viccars, my editor at David & Charles.
Thanks also to Julia Hiles, Kate Spiers and the staff of the British Library.*

*(Page 1) The repair gang (Hulton Deutsch)
(Page 2) 'When I grow up I want to be…' A young boy examining No 4482 Golden Eagle
at a railway exhibition at New Barnet in 1937 (Hulton Deutsch)
(Page 3) Still going strong on the Isle of Man: a 2–4–0 tank engine dating back to 1895*

*Colour and line illustrations by Philip Murphy
except pages 71, 72, 74, 75 and 126–32*

A DAVID & CHARLES BOOK

First published in the UK in 1998
Reprinted 1998, 1999, 2001, 2004
First paperback edition 2004

Copyright © Tom Quinn 1998, 2004

Tom Quinn has asserted his right to be identified as author of this work in accordance
with the Copyright, Designs and Patents Act, 1988.

A catalogue record for this book is available from the British Library.

ISBN 0 7153 0544 1 hardback
ISBN 0 7153 1687 7 paperback

Typeset by ABM Typographics Ltd Hull
Printed in China by SNP Leefung
for David & Charles
Brunel House   Newton Abbot   Devon

Visit our website at www.davidandcharles.co.uk

David & Charles books are available from all good bookshops; alternatively you can
contact our Orderline on (0)1626 334555 or write to us at FREEPOST EX2110, David &
Charles Direct, Newton Abbot, TQ12 4ZZ (no stamp required UK mainland).

CONTENTS

Introduction   7

CARDS & CHARACTERS: *Reg Coote: Driver on the Southern Railway*   15

HIGH DAYS AT HOLLOWAY: *George Case: Signalman on the*
London & North Eastern Railway   33

GENTLEMEN AT THE TOP!: *Richard Hardy: Shedmaster on the*
London North Eastern Railway   49

BRITAIN'S OLDEST RAILWAYMAN: *Vinsun Gulliver: Driver on the*
London Midland & Scottish and the London & North Eastern Railways   65

IN THE SIDINGS   70

THE BRAKE VAN MAN: *John Kerley: Guard on the*
London & North Eastern Railway   77

MEMORIES OF GREASE CORNER: *Bill Sidwell: Engineer on the*
London Midland & Scottish Railway   89

FROM FIREMAN TO FOREMAN: *Ray Beeson: Driver on the Southern Railway*   103

A COUNTRY STATIONMASTER: *Cliff Carr: Stationmaster on the*
London Midland & Scottish Railway   115

IN THE SIDINGS   126

STEAM IN THE BLOOD: *Jim McClelland: Driver on the*
London Midland & Scottish Railway   133

THE PEOPLE'S PORTER: *Tom Jales: Porter on the London North Eastern Railway*   145

EIGHTY YEARS A RAILWAYMAN: *Harry Horn: Signalman on the*
Great Western Railway   157

WORKING THE SADDLEBACKS: *Sandy Begg: Driver on the*
London & North Eastern Railway   167

A PILLAR OF THE COMMUNITY: *Rod Lock: Stationmaster on the*
London & North Eastern Railway   179

Index   189

Full steam ahead for the 1932 Christmas holidays: one of the numerous special trains which left Euston LMS station with passengers for the north (Hulton Deutsch)
(Opposite) A female worker on diesel shunter construction in the early 1950s (Derby Museums & Art Gallery Industrial Museum)

INTRODUCTION

People tend to become enthusiastic about the industrial past only when it is long gone; old mine workings, mills, pits and factories were far from entrancing when they were part of the everyday scene, and few waxed lyrical about them until long after they had been consigned to history. This is true of almost every industrial artefact one can imagine, with a single exception: the steam train.

Almost from the date of its invention the steam train was seen as a symbol of the liberating achievements of the industrial revolution. Even in its heyday when the steam locomotive was a common sight as it huffed and puffed its way into every corner of the land, it remained a thing of wonder, a thing of legend and romance. Landowners and others may have objected to the new railroads crossing their land, but the steam train's benefits to the vast bulk of the populace were so great that their objections were usually over-ridden.

Every youngster wanted to be a train driver when he grew up. It meant he would be master of a piece of machinery that seemed almost alive; it meant he would be in charge of a living, breathing thing of colossal power. Those old photographs of drivers standing proudly by their machines really do show the sense of pride the men had in their work. And this sense of pride was based not only on their own belief in what they could do, but on their awareness of the awe in which they were held by train passengers and the general public.

In the public imagination at least, the driver was the most important figure, probably closely followed by the stationmaster (this would certainly be true in smaller country

The tunnel rats (Hulton Deutsch)

stations); however, to reach the position of driver entailed a long apprenticeship – perhaps as long as fifteen years – first as cleaner and then fireman, before one was finally given the ultimate responsibility. Yet despite the long apprenticeship there was a curious informality about the route to promotion; thus a fireman would be expected to become familiar with driving simply by virtue of being with a driver, so that by the time he got an official 'turn' he was well versed in all the necessary procedures.

Certainly train driving was, and is, a highly responsible job: quite apart from the dangers of animals on the line, signals snowed under or trains derailed up ahead, the driver was wholly responsible for operating the locomotive correctly so as to ensure smooth, safe and punctual running, and this at a time when a locomotive boiler could be seriously damaged or even blow up if the driver and firemen made a serious mistake. By contrast, the modern train driver is a man who simply pushes the right buttons to get the engine to work. He doesn't have to rely on years of skill and experience to drive, though of course his level of responsibility is just as great as it was in the old days.

The pride with which locomotives were built, the intense competition to break speed records, and the competition among drivers to be the best and most punctual, all added to and sustained the sense that working on the railway was something out of the ordinary. Of course, steam involved a great deal more than driving. Signalmen, firemen, guards, shed-masters, stationmasters, platelayers and many others all played a part in a travel system that, until the Beeching cuts of the 1960s, was the finest in the world.

The magic of the steam railway stems in large part, I suspect, from the folk memory of how, within a few decades of its invention, the steam train had transformed the British Isles from a place of remote, isolated villages where only the very rich could afford to travel, to a place where travel for the masses became an affordable reality. A journey that might have taken four days by stagecoach in the 1830s could be completed just twenty years later in under a day. That is the true measure of the railway revolution and the sense of freedom it created; a sense that industry and its products *could* be truly liberating.

From the very earliest days, the railway also captured the imagination of poets, writers and artists. J. M. W. Turner's *Rain, Steam, and Speed – the Great Western Railway* (painted some time before 1844) is perhaps still the greatest artistic expression of the irresistible force of the new invention. Here the locomotive roars out of the mist towards us like a fire-breathing monster, and Nature – in the form of the barely visible hare limping away across the track – can only try to keep out of its way. In this century poets as diverse as Edward Thomas, John Betjeman, Philip Larkin and Stephen Spender have described the railway or used it metaphorically. Edward Thomas's 'Adlestrop' is one of the best-known examples, and it perfectly captures the loneliness of a remote country station:

> Yes. I remember Adlestrop –
> The name, because one afternoon
> Of heat the express-train drew up there
> Unwontedly. It was late June.
>
> The steam hissed. Someone cleared his throat.
> No one left and no one came
> On the bare platform. What I saw
> Was Adlestrop – only the name.
>
> And willows, willow-herb and grass,
> And meadowsweet, and haycocks dry,
> No whit less still and lonely fair
> Than the high cloudlets in the sky.
>
> And for that minute a blackbird sang
> Close by, and round him, mistier,
> Farther and farther, all the birds
> Of Oxfordshire and Gloucestershire.

By contrast, the inexorable power of the train is beautifully captured in Stephen Spender's *The Express*, while W. H. Auden tries to capture the very rhythm of the train in his *Night Mail*:

> This is the night mail crossing the Border,
> Bringing the cheque and the postal order.
> Letters for the rich, letters for the poor,
> The shop at the corner, the girl next door.

WAY
OUT

PARCELS &
CLOAKROOM

A classic 3F 0–6–0, produced at
Derby locomotive works, seen here
at Glastonbury on the Somerset &
Dorset Railway (Milepost)

INTRODUCTION

The nineteenth-century novel is rich in railway imagery and description, too: Mrs Gaskell, Charles Dickens and Thackeray among others are filled with references, and some of the most memorable passages from the works of these writers appear in the 'In the Sidings' section of this book. Because steam lasted until relatively recently – certainly well into the 1960s – we are very lucky in that a large number of individual steam railwaymen are still with us. Few have memories that go back quite as far as those of Vinsun Gulliver, however, whom I interviewed shortly before his 109th birthday – in 1996 he was the oldest man in Britain – and I was delighted to discover that he still remembered starting work on the railways in 1907. (Sadly, Vinsun died before this book could be published.)

But thousands of younger men, in their sixties, seventies and eighties, also remember working as part of a transport system that, in essentials, dated back to the 1840s and 1850s, to the earliest days of rail travel.

Before Stephenson's *Locomotion* appeared on the Stockton and Darlington Railway in 1825 heralding the dawn of the steam age, railways had existed in some form for centuries; indeed we know that wagons pulled by horses on wooden rails had been in use in industry, particularly mines, since at least the fourteenth century. Flanged wheels were one of the innovations that preceded the introduction of mechanical propulsion: they were introduced in 1789. From then on they were used throughout heavy industry, although the wagons continued to be horse-drawn until the beginning of the nineteenth century.

After the Stockton and Darlington, there was no stopping the railway: by the end of the 1830s some 1,500 miles of track had been laid in Britain; by 1885 that figure had reached nearly 17,000 miles; and by 1921 it was over 19,000 miles.

By 1921 Britain's 250 private railway companies were grouped into four regional companies: London Midland and Scottish Railways (LMS), London and North Eastern Railway (LNER), Great Western Railway (GWR) and Southern Railway (SR). In 1947 came nationalisation and the new name, British Railways, which in 1965 became British Rail. Now, of course, the whole thing has come full circle and the railways have been split into a number of privately owned companies once again. This book makes no attempt to deal with the technical or commercial side of the age of steam, except insofar as these matters affected the lives of individual railwaymen. It is not really a book for railway experts, although I hope even the most ardent enthusiast will enjoy it; instead it is an attempt simply to record the personal memories of a group of railwaymen who worked in different parts of the country and in different jobs. The book is designed to be both a tribute to these men and an attempt to record the details of their experiences in an extraordinary and fascinating world that has gone forever.

A note on the text
Each railwayman's main job is given at the head of the relevant chapter, but as drivers invariably started as cleaners, signalmen as messenger boys, and so on, readers will find that the book covers a far wider range of employment than might otherwise appear.

(Opposite) Loading coal onto an LMS tender (Hulton Deutsch)

CARDS & CHARACTERS

REG COOTE

Driver on the Southern Railway

Now seventy-three, Reg Coote started work on the Southern Railway in 1941. Like most railwaymen from the days of steam he can remember the exact date: 10 February, and like many retired steam railwaymen he remains in touch with large numbers of his ex-colleagues. In the old days, of course, workers were not always on the friendliest terms with management, but retirement has changed all that, as Reg explains:

'I know you're going to interview Richard Hardy – well, though we get on well now, we used to have some terrific barneys when we worked together. He was management and I was prominent in the union at local level, but in those days – and we both knew it – I had to be against everything he said!'

Before his railway career began, Reg had a colourful, if short-lived career on a Thames wherry or sailing barge – indeed, he must be one of the last men to have worked these traditional boats up and down the Thames. He spent the first year of his life in Egypt where he was born in 1924, the son of an airforceman. His father was born in Westminster towards the end of the nineteenth century while his mother came from Lambeth.

'I'm a real Londoner and so are all my family,' he says with a grin, 'and I have to admit I was a bit rough, too, in my early days!' Because his father was in the forces, Reg's school days were disrupted, and he moved from one school to another, never staying in one place for more than a few terms. By the time he was eleven, however, his father had retired from the Air Force and some semblance of order returned to Reg's life. He attended Lambeth School for Boys until he was fourteen, and has always regretted that he then had to leave.

'I had to leave as soon as I could because my dad had died six months after retiring from the Air Force – he was only forty-five – and Mum was short of money: everyone was short of money back then, in the 1930s. I sometimes feel a bit sad about my lack of education because in my last year I was top in most subjects.'

Reg's only connection with the railway at this time was a cousin, a driver, who lodged with the family at their home in Queen's Road, Battersea. At fourteen, of course, Reg was too young to go straight on to the railways anyway, so he took the first alternative offered to him: third hand on *The Thistle*, an old sailing barge, known as an ironside among the bargees. She'd been made in Glasgow but mostly plied the Thames.

'We used to go to Rowhedge near Colchester to collect sand,' he recalls. 'It was during the Munich crisis of 1938 that this all started. The sand we were bringing up to London was for sandbags – I reckon old Chamberlain was stalling for time with that bit of paper. We were hopelessly unprepared, and I think Chamberlain knew it. I discovered just how bad things were when I worked on the footplate during the war years. Coal and armaments were always in short supply and I remember my brother telling me that at Territorial Army meetings thirty blokes often had to share one rifle – and that was just months before war broke out!'

Reg spent long periods away from home working on the barge, and although the pay was poor he had little time to think about alternatives: 'It was a twenty-four-hour-a-day job, and if the wind happened to be blowing in the wrong direction we could be stuck indefinitely, miles from anywhere, or in some distant port because the boat had no engine as a back-up.'

Eventually, fed up with the uncertainties of life on the river, Reg began to listen to the stories of the railway told by his cousin: 'Well, he was always telling me it was a good job, and as he was my cousin and also our lodger I took my chance when it came up. The war was on by then, and in my last months on the barge I can remember watching the fiery glow of a big City seed-cake mill burning after being hit by bombs. We watched in astonishment from the river.'

Reg's cousin worked at Stewart's Lane, Battersea, a depot just down the road from the family home. Originally there had been two depots here: Battersea Park, which served the London Brighton and South Coast, and Battersea which served Chatham and Dover. In the 1920s they were amalgamated into what was called Stewart's Lane, and that's where Reg started his railway life, with five others, on 10 February 1941.

'I'd spent two years on the river,' he explains, 'and by this stage London was being heavily bombed. I remember being given a travel pass and a letter telling me to report to London Bridge for my medical; but when I got there, most of the area had been destroyed by bombs. Anyway, I had the medical and an intelligence test – as far as I can remember, to pass this you had to be able to answer just one question: "What is your name?"'

Reg has a marvellously irreverent view of his past, which explains why much of his conversation is sprinkled with wonderful stories and anecdotes. In fact among retired railwaymen Reg is something of a legend; but like so many youngsters who started on the railways in those days, his first job was as a cleaner: 'The three cleaner foremen that our little group of six new lads worked for were all in their forties; they seemed ancient to us, and it was a

reminder of just how long it took in the 1930s – when there were few jobs around – to get promoted!'

On that first day the new recruits were given a little safety lecture and a rule book, and were then taken into the stores. There they were each given two pairs of navy blue overalls and Reg, as the oldest in the group, was made ganger, the man in charge.

'I remember my chest swelling with pride!' he recalls with a grin. 'Being ganger meant I was in charge of the big red board with the white lettering on it! This read "Not to be Moved" and I had to place it on the lamp at the rear of every engine we cleaned while we were cleaning it. The board was supposed to stop us getting killed by some lunatic moving the train while we were underneath cleaning the motionwork. It might sound unlikely that someone could make a mistake like this, but while you were underneath the loco where a lot of the work needed to be done, you couldn't be seen because some of these engines were massive.'

Engines had to be cleaned thoroughly, and it was up to the new recruits to do the job well enough for the loco to 'pass muster' under the eyes of an inspector who would simply make them do it all again if it was not up to scratch. Reg is typically lighthearted about the whole thing:

'We must have been a pretty sight covered in oil half the time, but even so, marching proudly around. We were all sixteen or seventeen, and as we trooped around the shed I always went first, carrying the board as if it was a military flag and followed by a lad carrying the oil in what we called a bottle (the oil smelled like cat's pee!); the next lad in the line carried the Vaseline for cleaning and someone else had the cotton waste, the wipes and rags we would use. The cleaner foremen showed us how to clean because it wasn't that straightforward and it had to be just right. Passenger engines had to be knobbed up a good bit more than goods, but they all had to pass the foreman's test. He'd come along and check underneath in all those little inaccessible places you might have thought you could get away with not cleaning at all.'

Pumice and brick-dust were used to make the metalwork shine in those pre-detergent days, and the first loco Reg remembers cleaning was the 21C, the first Merchant Navy class: 'That would have been the end of 1941,' he recalls, 'and I remember the paintwork was so rough it shredded our rags – absolutely tore them to bits!'

Under normal circumstances cleaners could look forward to many years in that relatively unelevated role, but the war had caused a severe shortage of manpower with the result that all the old ways disappeared almost overnight, and men were promoted very quickly

indeed. 'Within six weeks of us starting work we were told: "You're going out as firemen". Proud as Punch we immediately went round scrounging caps from older firemen,' remembers Reg.

In those days the railway workers were represented by two powerful unions and they both tried to recruit youngsters as soon as they could. 'I remember on our first pay-day we got snapped up by ASLEF,' says Reg. 'They were on to us like a shot, but it could just as easily have been the NUR; it was just that on that particular Friday the ASLEF man happened to be quicker off the mark. I remember the ASLEF rep was a driver called Alf Murray who, as it happens, only died recently, in his nineties. But we were in touch almost till the end, which just shows how railwaymen stick together.'

Cleaners at Stewart's Lane, as elsewhere, had their own lobby – a sort of common room – and in those days it was completely separate from the drivers' and firemens' lobby. Job demarcation was rigid, as Reg explains: 'Once you were a fireman or driver you never went in the cleaners' room and they never came in ours. I remember all the lobby windows were covered with tar because of the blackout, and there was always a huge open fire; and it had a long table with a two-inch thick top and a wooden form – a bit like a school bench – which was bolted to the floor just in case you might walk out with it under your arm!'

Thrown into the deep end at virtually no notice and in a way that was all but unprecedented in the railway industry, Reg and his four mates were given no training before taking up their duties as firemen. For weeks on end they were put on one of the most arduous shifts, 8pm to 4am, and with a number of different drivers. None of this would have happened but for the war. When the lads weren't firing they did shed work, cleaning smokeboxes and fireboxes, loading the trains with coal and water and turning the engines round.

'It was bloody hard work,' remembers Reg. 'On the King Arthur class the clinker shovel was some fifteen feet long – you imagine lifting that with a great heavy lump of clinker on the end! Clinker is different from coal; it's the dirt from the coal really, I suppose. Cleaning out the fire (as opposed to the clinker) means you're moving coal that's still burning. Under all the fire and the clinker there were the ash pans, the dampers and the smokebox to clean.

'On the old goods engines you'd sometimes open the fire door and find another door, of solid ash! Moving that was a filthy job and all the dirt used to get into your clothes – it was so bad that all the cleaners wore bicycle clips: at least that stopped it going up your trouser legs! I always wore a big red spotted handkerchief round my neck, too. Without these precautions you'd have so much dirt on you it would take a week to get it off!'

Reg was officially designated a fireman cleaner, but after a while his main work centred on firing engines – getting them ready from cold – in the yard. He worked on what the Stewart's Lane men called pilot or shunting engines. These were used to break up and make up trains: six carriages here, ten there, whatever was needed.

'We worked on ammunition trains – and there were a lot of those, I can tell you – as well as troop trains and tank trains. The tank trains were interesting; they'd be made up as follows: you'd get two locomotives one behind the other at the front (you'd need that sort of power because of the weight of the tanks) followed by a coach for the officers, then a coach for the men, then flatbeds for the tanks, then another coach. When we used two engines we called it a double header.

'We also used to move trains around a lot to keep the Germans guessing. I can recall a couple of these trains made up with each flatbed loaded with giant papier-mâché guns – the

Reg's favourite engine, the E1 converted copper top

idea was that from the air, the Germans would think we were incredibly well equipped, although the opposite was true.

'The railway helped with some great tricks in the war; for instance, down at Dover we had one massive gun, a real one this time, mounted on the railway, and this was used to lob shells regularly over the Channel. When it fired it would quickly reverse through a long tunnel, pop out the other side and fire again, so old Gerry thought we had two big guns there, not just one!'

During this period Reg was on what was known as a 'P and D' gang: for the preparation and disposal of trains at the start and end of their working days. The drivers in the shed were called red carders, meaning that they could drive, but only in the shed; they were never allowed to drive outside. Cleaner firemen such as Reg on the P and D gangs were passed cleaners, that is, cleaners who fired at least some of the time. The drivers in the shed, on the other hand, were passed firemen.

'It was as if, when you moved up the promotion ladder, the description of what you did was there to remind you of what you *had* done – so a passed cleaner was really a fireman in all but name. I was firing on the shunting engines for some years. I was a member of the Norwood Harriers, so called – unofficially, of course – because we were always racing

between Battersea and Norwood. During this period I met one of the funniest men I've ever met; he was known as Monty, and he could do the most brilliant impersonations of film stars. He used to keep us entertained for hours, and during the war years that was just what we needed.'

Among the worst jobs a young fireman had to cope with was firing the W-class engines: 'They were horrible,' says Reg with a grimace, 'because they effectively had three engines – one on either side and one underneath, so they had to be oiled up from underneath, which was hot and filthy.'

As in most occupations where a group of people have to work together closely and who rely heavily on each other, railway workers always had nicknames. In fact it was almost universal, unless – as in Reg's own case – your name was already considered to be something of a nickname: 'Well, being called Coote I didn't have a chance, did I? Most of my mates thought Coote was my nickname and that I had another real name, but such was the liking for nicknames I was also known as skipper.

'Sometimes people had nicknames for odd reasons – one bloke was called Charlie because he hated his real name, which was Monty, and we had lots of Smiths so I suppose they had to have nicknames to distinguish them one from another: there was Big Bill Smith who was about seven feet tall, Two Gun Smith because he was always playing with an air pistol, Dab Toes Smith who walked in an odd way, and Holy Joe who was a lay preacher. When Holy Joe was on the footplate he used to make me laugh: if the train seemed to be going too fast to stop easily he'd put his hands up in the air and shout, "Don't worry! The Lord will provide!" After he retired he went to live in Bath and got a job as a lollipop man, and he was famous for leaping out in front of oncoming vehicles regardless of the risk and shouting, "The Lord will provide!"

'Yes, there were hundreds of characters and only a few miserable unfriendly so-and-sos,' says Reg with a huge grin.

Becoming a passed cleaner or passed fireman was really a question of being allowed – usually temporarily at first – to cover holidays and sickness, in the job above the one you normally did. But to reach this stage you had to do enough 'turns' to qualify.

'After we'd had thirteen turns firing we were entitled to an overcoat, or "P"-jacket as we called it. That was a sort of dufflecoat, but it was a sign that you were a passed fireman. After 313 turns – that's a whole year, not including Sundays – you got a serge jacket and a brass cap badge. Then you'd really arrived, but if I remember correctly you could get round the system by paying the storeman ten bob and he'd flog you a brass cap badge. I couldn't afford to buy my badge, and this was awkward because sometimes you'd get an old stickler of a driver who wouldn't let you on the footplate without it.'

The fireman had a great deal of responsibility on the footplate, basically making sure that things were ready for when the driver arrived. The routine would be as follows: at the start of a shift the fireman would climb up onto the footplate and immediately make sure he had everything he needed: shovel, brush, coal-pick, bucket, spanners, flare lamps, four headlights each with a red shade, and three disc boards or targets. He would put these disc boards on the front of the train so the signalmen could see the train's code. Then the driver would arrive. At this stage it became something of a team effort, as Reg explains:

'If he was keen the driver would get the oil; if not, you did it. We always had a big oil bottle and a small one. The big oil bottle had thin engine oil which had to be applied to various points. The driver did the actual oiling. The small oil bottle had a thicker, black oil. Before you set off you'd prepare the fire and check the sandbox – if the train slipped on the rails you could allow the sand to trickle onto the rail to help the wheels grip. Lots of engines were what we called "tippy-toey" which meant they would slip at the least provocation, so sand was essential – and woe betide if you went off without it! Oh, and I should also mention that some regions had what were called fire droppers – the men who got the fire going in the engine from cold – but we firemen did this at Battersea. Anyway, having checked the sand, we'd also check that we were OK for water, and would then toot four for Victoria (if that was where we were going), two for Herne Hill and five for Victoria Central. This was to let the signalman know what was what.'

To some extent drivers and firemen were a law unto themselves during the steam era. Yet despite what many people might now judge to be slightly unorthodox practices, accidents were extremely rare.

'We never had any major accidents – at least none I knew about – although there were one or two slip-ups: men used to hitch a ride on the footplate, for example. This wouldn't be allowed now, and it was, strictly speaking, illegal to do this even then, but people turned a blind eye to it. You might get half a dozen of your mates going to Victoria like this. Well, once we had a pack of them on the footplate and as luck would have it the train they were on went over a set of points that were all wrong – wrecked the points and caused a fuss, but no serious damage. And I remember once on the 3am paper train a bunch of men were going home on the footplate and they were chatting away so merrily that they didn't notice the fireman had gone to make a cup of tea before they set off. They'd set off without him!

He had to catch the next paper train and I hate to think what he said when he caught up with the others!'

Like a great many railwaymen, Reg was in a reserved occupation, although he did try to join up when war started. He told the recruiting sergeant he was a shed sweeper (not a reserved occupation), received his initial army pay and was told to report for duty in four weeks.

'We were supposed to go in the Royal Armoured Corps,' he recalls. 'When I told my mum she fainted because my dad had only recently died and my brother was away fighting. Anyway, she secretly contacted the army and told them what my real job was. When I got to Beverley in Yorkshire where I'd been told to report I was immediately called out and sent home with a day's ration money. I've still got my service card which says one day's service, twenty-eight days' leave, and reason for discharge, "Services no longer required". I was damn lucky, too, 'cos I got 3s 6d a day for my twenty-eight days' leave.'

Inevitably Reg's memories of the war years are especially vivid. Partly, of course – and as he is the first to admit – this has a lot to do with the camaraderie instilled by the sense of shared danger, for the railways were a prime target for German bombers. But if train driving was a dangerous job in those days it had huge compensations, not least the wide range of characters and individualists who made up the workforce.

'During the last months of the war I was firing for a driver called Sammy Jingle. He was a real character, and a terror for the throttle – it used to be said of him that he'd set every cornfield alight as he went along; that's how much the sparks used to fly when he was in charge! But Sammy knew all the roads, and we used to work the army leave trains down at Dover on the south coast. I remember all the soldiers were absolutely loaded down with booty – German swords, helmets and souvenirs of every description, till the customs people stopped it. We were working a King Arthur class engine at this time with thirteen coaches: twelve, plus one for the NAAFI.'

Other wartime journeys took Reg to Gravesend where German prisoners were landed in their tens of thousands. 'They were locked into the coaches and hadn't washed for months; the smell was indescribable. I remember, too, that early in the war these prisoners were great big strapping Bavarian types, very proud even though they were prisoners, but towards the end we were collecting boys and old men. You'd see kids in uniform – they were twelve and thirteen and usually in tears. There were old men, too – Hitler didn't care who he called up in the end. All along the road as we took the train across from Gravesend to Kempton there were British soldiers on the bridges overhead carrying machine guns. We drove two and three trainloads a day for weeks on end.

'On the ambulance trains they would often carry out major operations, amputations and so on. I remember we used to be handed boxes by the medical staff to throw in the firebox and we were convinced they contained legs and arms. An SS man I spotted being carried along on a stretcher had a leg and an arm removed and he was still sitting bolt upright on the stretcher giving the Nazi salute with his one remaining arm. All this helped with the shortages, however. I remember saying I needed a pair of boots, and next minute a tea-chest arrived full of boots!'

At a time when Britain's population was suffering from severe shortages of everything from clothing to food, the railwayman's lot could occasionally be a happy one, and never more so than when well-fed American troops began to arrive.

Refitting at Ashford works: No 302 Ashford works crane locomotive, built in 1881 by Neilson & Co

'When the Yanks first came over we had to move them around the country and as soon as we'd dropped a load of them off, we used to go straight into the carriages to collect up the ration boxes they always left all over the place. The boxes each contained one meal for a man, together with chewing gum, chocolate and even condoms! The chocolate was horrible, but to us poor half-starved devils the fact that most of the boxes were left untouched was a wonderful bonus.'

Many railwaymen were killed during German air-raids, and important railway offices sometimes had their headquarters inside tunnels; the shedmaster at Orpington in Kent, for example, worked in an office in an old, disused one. The tunnels were useful in other ways, too – for instance, if a train was buzzed by enemy aircraft the driver and fireman would race for the nearest tunnel, as Reg did on a number of occasions.

'I worked with a driver called Bill Murray during the war years – another great character – and once when we were heading for Brighton we were buzzed by a German plane. We were in the second engine of a double header and you've never seen anything like the spurt we put on – despite the weight of a hell of a lot of carriages – to get to the nearest tunnel.

We suddenly found we had the strength of ten men – that's what fear does to you! Anyway, we waited hours in the tunnel till we thought it was safe to come out, and finally arrived in Brighton at 4am. We were taking a load of Scottish troops to the coast, and when they marched out of the station at 4am I've always wondered what the locals made of the fact that they insisted on a full pipe band playing full blast at the head of the column!'

But with the end of the war came other occasional distractions, such as more visitors from abroad, more holidaymakers and sometimes VIPs. Reg was once even ejected from the footplate by a young VIP, as he recalls:

'I was firing on a Golden Arrow – can't remember when, but it was probably in 1947 – when an inspector came onto the footplate and said, "You've got a VIP aboard, so watch it!" When we arrived at Victoria we were told the VIP wanted to come onto the footplate. As the fireman I had to make myself scarce, and then up popped a twelve-year-old boy! I couldn't believe it when they told me he was the King of Iraq! Still, I got ten bob for my pains.'

Despite the fears and excitements of the wartime years, railway work was never very well paid and, like many men, Reg looked about after the end of hostilities for better-paid alternative occupations.

'Yes, I nearly packed it all in, the money was so poor. The pay was about £6 a week. That sounds quite good when you think I'd started in 1941 on £1 6s 2d, most of which I had to give to my mum. But that £6 was very low after the war and I thought that lots of other jobs would probably pay a lot more. I suppose it really was love of the work that kept me at it, and the fact that all my mates were railwaymen. Mind you, having complained about the pay I ought to admit that we all wasted a lot of money gambling. The Battersea men were terrible gamblers. I didn't get too involved, except once when I lost my whole wage packet, only to win it back at the last minute. But the stress involved in that put me off for a long time! During the war years a lot of the gambling came about as a result of troop moving, because we were kept hanging around for ages and gambling was one way to fill the time.'

Reg is an excellent storyteller with a keen memory for detail and, with his jolly, animated face and gravelly voice, he is skilled at bringing the past to life again, clearly relishing the memory of former triumphs and disasters. He fired on the Golden Arrow boat service for many years after the war, and in 1948 passed for driving. In terms of everyday work this meant little change for Reg as, like all firemen with years of experience, he'd done hundreds of turns as a driver already. The only real change was an increase in wages. Driving, like firing, was a question of knowing exactly what you had to do, and when.

'After a while you got into a routine and everything would go like clockwork. One driver I worked with is a good example. He never wore a watch, yet every time we took a train to Ashford – an hour from Victoria – the minute hand on the station platform clock would move from 59 to 60 minutes just as we pulled into the platform.

'Once I passed for driving I never went firing again, except perhaps at Christmas when you stayed in your grade – in other words, when you dropped back a grade. After the war there was very little work in winter so we spent a lot of time in the pub; and then in summer it was non-stop because all the soldiers were back, they had money and they wanted to go on holiday. There was a train out of Victoria every ten minutes for holidaying soldiers. Some were day excursions, too; it was as if, the war being over, everyone was absolutely determined to celebrate. Firms organised outings for their workers, too; they'd always have a bar and send up beer to us men on the footplate.'

Throughout his long years of service Reg never lost his enjoyment of the actual process of driving, and like most drivers he enjoyed a challenge, as he explains:

'I enjoyed driving goods trains more than passenger, simply because there was more to it. Goods trains were sometimes so long that at any one time the train might be on three levels: the front going slightly uphill, the middle on the level and the back going downhill. The wagons had no brakes, either, so with that much behind you, you sometimes put the brake down and left it and just hoped for the best! But you can imagine how you had to concentrate on what you were doing, with that much going on behind you!' And if the work itself could be varied and demanding, so too could the engines the men had to work with.

'The West Country class Golden Arrow trains we used had some interesting peculiarities, as did every engine. In fact they were all individuals. You always had to remember to watch the water because if there was too much, the brake would come on automatically.

'Most of all I enjoyed driving the boat trains on the Ostend route. During the war a fireman was earning about 9s 6d a day, and that would go up by a tanner a year until he got to the top rate which was 11s 6d. A driver got 15s a day, but if he'd only recently passed as a driver he had to work terrible shifts. Goods was all-night work, for example.

'By 1955 I was working on steam and on the new electric lines – they'd electrified the Ramsgate line in about 1959. At first the electric seemed great – so clean after steam, and you got better shifts; but it changed the whole atmosphere of the thing. By 1961 they'd electrified the Ostend boat train and the Golden Arrow had become an electric engine.'

In addition to his firing and driving work, Reg put a great deal of time into union work throughout his career: 'I was always keen on the union, and for many years was assistant branch secretary for Battersea. We used to organise dinner dances and a huge kids' party every Christmas; this was held in a big listed building in Vauxhall in central London, the Brunswick Building, which is still there. I can remember carting hundreds of party hats and jellies around the streets of south London in a mate's old car, and being terrified we might squash them all!'

Time off in the Dewdrop pub in Battersea – Reg is at the back, second from the left

One of Reg's most poignant memories is of the solidarity of railwaymen at difficult times. They stood up for each other and helped the widows and orphans of dead colleagues. Funerals of colleagues were treated with due respect, and woe betide a man who failed to do his bit.

'When a driver died in the steam days his mates were always the pallbearers. They carried the coffin out of his house to the horse-drawn hearse – everyone insisted on horses in those days – and the whole street came out to

A period Southern Railway scene from the late 1940s: Tangmere, *a fine example of the new streamlined Light Pacifics* (Milepost)

see the coffin away. The chapel would be packed out with his mates, too. I remember old Bill Cook died at Stewart's Lane, and you couldn't move in the church. But that sort of thing faded out with the coming of the electric, and then diesel.

'The best way to illustrate the change is probably to compare the way we made collections for a dead man's widow at the start of my career and the way we had to do it towards the end of my time. In the old days when a man died we'd leave a tin out in the lobby to collect money for the relatives, and no one would have even dreamt of doing anything other than adding to the amount already in the tin; but towards the end we had to stop doing it because all the money got stolen. That would never have happened in the steam days.'

Reg is no starry-eyed nostalgic, however: he enjoyed the steam days, but he was, and is, well aware of their limitations. For instance, demarcation was strict and men in different grades often ignored each other: 'In the drivers' lobby or common room the Chatham men would sit at one end with the Brighton blokes at the other and they'd *never* talk to each other. And men in different areas tried to keep themselves apart from everyone else – the drivers at Nine Elms, for example, always wore dickey bows. It was a way of saying who they were, and if they met another man with a dickey bow, of course, they knew instantly they were mates. This is probably why the men at each depot had group nicknames, too, like the Dover Sharks and the Old Kent Roaders!'

Reg in the cab!

But drivers and firemen were sticklers for tradition and for not forgetting their friends. Near Gillingham in Kent, where Reg decided to live in retirement and where he still lives today, an old driver he'd once known, called Dizzy Farrow, is buried; and for years after he died every driver coming along the track by the graveyard would toot Dizzy as they went by.

'Drivers definitely thought they were a class above the rest, and they were very militant as a result,' remembers Reg. But rivalries between drivers and firemen were as nothing to the rivalries between men and management.

'Management and unions used to meet for discussions at a hotel in Somerset. The idea was that we could have brain-storming sessions well away from the "us and them" environment where discussions normally took place. To make this even easier you were never told what the other people in your group did back at work. This was so you could say what you really thought without worrying about who you were saying it to. It also meant you could end up sitting next to someone really very senior indeed. I remember being in charge of my group and one bloke – he was a bit snotty – didn't take part; so I had a go at him, only to discover that he was one of the most important people in the whole railway industry! Still, I never got into trouble over it.'

If Reg's memories are anything to go by, railway work attracted and bred wonderful characters who got up to all sorts of entertaining mischief. Dizzy Farrow, the driver buried at Gillingham, is a case in point, as Reg recalls:

'We were in the drivers' lobby, all sitting around the long table by the fire, when Dizzy Farrow – he'd be over a hundred now if he was still alive – started arguing with his mate about some obscure subject; and then suddenly Dizzy leaps up, grabs a milk bottle and some bits of paper and sets up an impromptu ouija-board. There must have been fifty or sixty blokes round that table watching half a dozen of their mates pushing this old milk bottle round with their fingertips asking: "Is there anyone with us tonight?" Just at the quietest moment, when we were all breathless with anticipation, some joker threw a detonator on the fire. You can imagine the mayhem when that went off – Dizzy jumped so high that he lost his hat and never found it!

'Another time we were gambling in the lobby when we saw a policeman's head peep through one of the blackout windows, and this gave us the fright of our lives because gambling in the lobby was illegal – but it was only old Rasher (can't remember his real name) taking the mickey. He shouted, "Stay where you are!" Thinking this really was a raid, someone else turned the light off and we all made a grab for the pile of money that had built up in the middle of the table. When the lights came on, all the money had gone!

'Another great character I fired for was Bert Hutton. He was a nice bloke but always in a bit of a mood on the down train – the early morning one – so I never used to say a word to him till we were on the up train later in the day. He was all right by then. Charlie Bird was another marvellous driver I worked with in my early days. He used to tell me that when I became a driver I was bound now and then to over-run a signal or go a bit past the platform, and that I'd need some standard answers for these misdemeanours. He then told me what he used to put on the enquiry forms. For lost time he'd fill in the form with the following, which I always thought very funny:

"The wind was high, the steam was low
The train was heavy and hard to tow
The coal was bad and mixed with slate
And that is why this train ran late."

'His second excuse was that – to quote him – "the tractive effort overcame the adhesive effort".

'One boastful driver I worked for was Sid Wickens; he was famous for boasting about everything under the sun, although he was a nice bloke all the same. We used to work together in the Haydon's Lane area where there was a pub we'd go to for our bread and cheese at lunchtime. Old Sid always used to have an onion with his lunch – he absolutely loved onions, and one day one of the pub regulars said to him, "I bet I've got an onion you can't eat". Well, ever boastful, old Sid said he could eat any onion in the world. So the two men bet a pint on it. Next day we were in the pub when this bloke comes in with the biggest onion I've ever seen in my life. I'm not joking – it was the size of a dinner plate. Sid wasn't going to be beaten, so he ate it all. He had his pint, and a pint from the man who'd brought the onion along, and back we went to work.

'A couple of hours later we came down Tulse Hill and stopped at the arrival signal where we usually had a ten-minute wait. As soon as we stopped Sid said, "Look after her", jumped out of the cab and disappeared across the tracks. I didn't see him again for two days and apparently he spent both of them in the loo!'

Reg's memories go back, in a sense, to the end of the nineteenth century, for the older men he worked with at the beginning of his career still talked about Victorian times and had distinctly Victorian habits: 'The old drivers used to hand round their snuffboxes,' he says, 'and some could barely read and write – I don't think it was felt to be important for a railwayman when they'd started work.'

By contrast, education and recreation – perhaps with the emphasis on the latter – had become an important element in railway life by the mid-1950s: 'We had regular educational outings during my time,' says Reg with a roar of laughter, 'though to be honest these tended to turn into a bit of a booze-up. But everyone loved them.

'We were all Chelsea supporters, and once I remember we went to Portsmouth for an away game. Afterwards we were all enjoying a drink outside a local pub when a bloke walked past with a small pony in tow. I don't know why, but we asked if we could buy the pony and its owner a drink. Next minute the pony was in the bar drinking beer out of a bucket! I remember that when we were about to set off home, the pony and his owner could be seen disappearing into the distance, but both swaying and weaving because they'd had a little too much. I remember how much we laughed because the owner had his arm round the pony's neck and we were convinced they were having a nice little chat.

'These outings grew in popularity and we even went to Amsterdam once – and when we went by train it was quite normal for the buffet car to have run out of alcohol by the time we were halfway there. A railwayman likes a drop, as they say!'

Working for the union probably made Reg a tougher, less sentimental railwayman than most, but he readily admits that with retirement he has mellowed: 'I never thought I was sentimental about the old days till I went to the Bluebell Railway, a restored steam line. As soon as I smelled the steam and the coal, I was in tears.'

But among all the happy memories Reg has one of near-disaster: 'I was only ever involved in one accident; I was seventeen at the time. We were on a 796 King Arthur class with Cecil Dudley driving, and we'd been given the road from Victoria; "Take this train to Chatham," they said, "and you'll be relieved there." We were supposed to leave at 8.40am, but as soon as we left the station we hit the 8.35 for Ramsgate – or rather, he hit us. He'd left for Clapham Road where he was supposed to wait and then come back to Victoria; in fact he'd gone out of the station to the first signal and then come back again – straight into us.

'I was looking out the window at the time. I saw a terrific flash, sparks and flames everywhere, and as this was wartime I thought we'd been hit by a bomb. What I'd actually seen was flames from the paraffin spilled when the headlamps were smashed. Cecil, my driver, hit the reverser, but in the confusion the brake handle dropped and cut his face badly. I smashed my leg on the water gauge.

'We couldn't get out at first because all the coal had come forward onto the blackout sheet and we were trapped under it. One of our buffers was found over by the central signal box a hundred yards away – if anyone had got in the way of *that* they'd have known about it! They had to cut the two engines apart. The poor old driver of the Ramsgate train had broken his pelvis and a few ribs. I remember, too, the Ramsgate fireman had two lovely black eyes because he'd been looking into the lubricator when the accident happened.

'There was a huge fuss over this accident. Anyway, they got us out and down to hospital, but I only suffered bad bruising. I was sent home, but my mother, a strict disciplinarian, thought I was trying to pull a fast one and she made me go back to work. I had to get a note from my guvn'r telling her that I had to be allowed to stay at home for a few days.

'I had five days off in total, and shortly after had to go to my brother's wedding in Harlow. I was best man and I remember I had to get permission not to kneel because I just couldn't. 'Coming up to London on the train these days I look across at Stewart's Lane and I think of all the days I spent there with my mates. They were my best days, and now all those men are retired or dead. It always brings a tear to my eye.'

HIGH DAYS AT HOLLOWAY

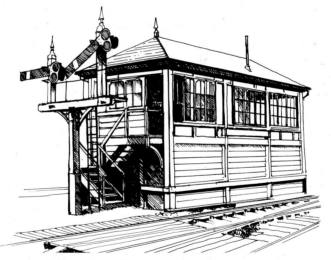

GEORGE CASE

*Signalman on the London &
North Eastern Railway*

'I used to sing to Ribbentrop, Goering and Goebbels,' says former signalman George Case with a grin. 'They came to Potters Bar as foreign dignitaries before the war when I was at school. They came each November for a service at St Mary's Church, Potters Bar, to pay homage to the Zeppelin crews shot down in the vicinity during the First World War!'

Surrounded by beautiful, large-scale model steam trains, George still lives in Potters Bar where he has spent most of his life. But he was born just a few miles away at Finsbury Park on the outskirts of London: 'I think we're an old Potters Bar family,' he says proudly, 'my father was born and lived all his life here.'

And railway work runs deep in the Case family. George's father was a guard for forty-five years – he started in 1917 – and his grandfather worked as a platelayer; George, seventy-two, still has his father's NUR card for 1918. He can remember family stories of the perils of Victorian days on the railway: 'It was a rough old job being on fogging duty in those days; my grandfather had to stand there for hours on end in the freezing cold with his flags and lamps so the drivers had some idea what was going on.' Tragically he was killed in Hadley Wood Tunnel, in Hertfordshire, while on fogging duty in 1918.

It might seem that, with so long a family connection with the railway, George's career choice would have been virtually made for him; but it was actually a little more complicated than that, as he explains:

'I wanted to go in the Navy, but my dad said "No", and my mum said she didn't want me on the railways. After that I did start to get interested in trains; in fact, I was eventually so interested that I used to sneak off from school up to Holloway North Up signal cabin, one of the biggest cabins in London, to see if I could find out how the whole thing worked. I was mad keen to learn signals, but I wasn't quite fourteen then and I was supposed to be at school – though I suppose my dad was quite good about it in the end. When he found out I'd been learning semaphore he got me a semaphore instrument, and he'd sit downstairs while I sat upstairs in my bedroom, and we'd send signals back and forth. We had great fun, but I also learned a lot.'

By this time the war had started, so George decided he'd join the railway; and after the time he had spent learning semaphore at home he was now committed to a career as a signalman:

'I went down to Holloway yardmaster's office. In those days you had to replace someone to get a job; in other words, if someone wanted to leave the railway, or if they were joining the Army, you could take their place. If they couldn't find someone they couldn't leave. A mate of mine wanted to go into the Air Force so I jumped at the chance to replace him as telegraph lad, which is exactly how my dad had started. I got a reference from the vicar at Potters Bar and a school reference. As a matter of interest my mate Leslie, the chap whose job I was to take, distinguished himself by being the first RAF man to shoot down a

A heavily loaded LNER lorry

Messerschmitt 109E, a plane that the British authorities were desperate to get a look at.'

George's father only realised that his son had left school after George had already been at work for a month – the school board man called at the house and the game was up.

'He was furious when he found out,' says George. 'He made me go back to school till I was legally allowed to leave and start work, which was on my fourteenth birthday, 14 November 1940. This meant going back for only a short time, however, and as soon as I could I went back to be a lad messenger. I started each day at 8.30am at Finsbury Park, and I had to go down to all the platelayers' cabins and signal cabins to pick up the mail for the yardmaster. I was a small boy and I had to carry a huge bag back and forth across the main lines – can you imagine being allowed to do that today! There were seven sets of lines and you just had to keep an eye out for the trains. If it was foggy they'd detail someone from the shunters' yard to see you across the rails. Once I'd collected all the mail I'd take it to the yardmaster's office, and open it ready for the chief clerk who would arrive at about 9am.'

The lad messenger was without question at the bottom of the pile, but as he dashed between various people doing different jobs George gained an insight into how all the parts of the railway worked. Apart from sorting out the post he had to look after the stores: 'I can remember taking massive blocks of soap out and cutting off huge chunks to cart to the various cabins. Then I had to deal with applications for privilege passes – these were reduced-fare tickets for railwaymen to travel. This was the London North Eastern (LNER) region so our forms were white.

'At 10.30am I had to make tea for the entire office staff, then I'd run messages for all and sundry. I even had to measure up the railwaymen for their uniforms – it must have been a funny sight. There I was, a little lad of fourteen or fifteen, pulling the tape measure round these huge men. All the railway uniforms at that date were supplied by Lotteries of Liverpool Street.'

Inevitably, as the newest and youngest recruit, George had to put up with a lot of practical jokes. He remembers being asked to get red oil for some lamps and green oil for others, and of course he fell for it and spent long periods looking for things that didn't exist. But occasionally the jokes backfired:

'I remember in my very early days going across the tracks to the platelayers' cabin at Holloway to see a Mr Hudson, also known as Soapy. When I got there he said "Casey," – they all called me Casey – "I want a privilege ticket. I want to go to Delhi". I said, "Do you mean Delhi in India?" and when he said "Yes", I believed him. I just said, "Oh, that'll be the pink form as it's outside our region". I asked him what route he wanted to take and everything – I don't know how he kept a straight face. Anyway, I made out the appropriate form and that afternoon the form went into the yardmaster's box.

'A short while later I heard the bell ringing violently to tell me that the guvn'r wanted me. He was a Mr Keys and I always remember how he wore a pince-nez on the end of his nose.

"Case," he said.

"Yes sir," I said.

"This application form from Mr Hudson."

"Yes, sir. His old aunt is sick and he wants to visit her," I said.

"Think you'd better get Hudson," he said.

'So I set off across the rails to the platelayers' cabin and found Hudson, who was a very big man, busy playing cards.

'I said, "Mr Keys wants to see you."

"What the bloody hell does he want," roared Hudson.

"It's about your privilege pass to Delhi."

'At that Hudson leapt to his feet and shouted.

"You haven't filled it out, have you, you silly bugger!"

'I could hear all sorts of bellowing from Mr Keys' office after Hudson went in, and he came out looking very sheepish. There were no more tricks like that afterwards.'

When George started work even a boy of fourteen was expected to do a forty-eight hour week. Each day finished at 5pm weekdays, and at noon on Saturdays, with half an hour for lunch. Occasionally George, like the other workers, would finish at ten past the hour, or ten to – 'I'm buggered if I can remember why!' he says.

George worked as a messenger boy for a total of only six months; during the war years, job changing and even promotion was far easier than it had been before the war, simply because of the shortage of men. 'I got myself a new job, but in the usual way of the time I had to get a replacement for my old job before I could move on. I was lucky, because I managed to get a friend called Mo Kantor to take my place as messenger boy. His dad was a furrier in Potters Bar and though you might have thought he'd have followed in his father's footsteps, he joined me on the railways. I taught him everything I knew in the messenger boy line, and then became a telegraph lad at Holloway, South Down Cabin.'

George's first wage packet contained just 14s 6d, but 2d of that disappeared immediately into what was then called the 'Lloyd George', an early unemployment tax. Despite getting himself a new job with extra responsibilities, George had to accept that he was not going to receive any more money. The rule on the railway was that you didn't get a pay rise, whatever you were doing, until your next birthday. Thereafter at each birthday you received a further 1s rise.

'They had a terrible initiation ceremony for all new entrants,' remembers George. 'They'd grab you when you went in the platelayers' cabin, sharpen a cut-throat razor right in front of you, and make it really look like they were going to cut your privates off!' However, having survived the perils of the platelayers' cabin intact, George was subsequently amazed to discover how much responsibility a fourteen-year-old was expected to cope with:

'You went straight into a signals cabin where you learned to fill in the train registration book. In a busy box you'd have 4 pages of booking per shift: each line of entry in the book had 10 items that had to be filled in – the time the train was offered, the time it was accepted, time passed on, time passing in the rear and so on. It worked out at 10 items per line, 40 lines per page: a total of 400 items per page, and there were 4 pages each shift!

'That was a hell of a lot of entries for a young lad. At the Holloway signal cabin I did 6am–2pm and 2pm–10pm shifts. You had to be there at 6am, and if you were the least bit late they knew straightaway because the bookings would not be there, and of course you couldn't add them after the event.'

Despite the heavy workload of the registration book there were other, equally onerous duties. George had to use the telephone, tap out telegraph messages, and once a week get down on his hands and knees to scrub the signalbox floorboards till they were white. The massive metal frame the levers were held in had to be black-leaded every week, too: 'Anyone who has ever done *that* will know what a filthy job it is. The black-leading used to get everywhere – on your clothes, up your nose, all over your face. But they wanted it to look smart and clean and well looked after, which it did. At Holloway there were fifty levers that had to be polished, too. Signalmen were always proud men, who wanted their cabins to be just right.'

Messages from the signalbox were sent up and down the line via the block bells – basically a brass bell in a mahogany case – and this, too, had to be kept sparklingly clean. 'Even the screw heads on all the bits of equipment were polished regularly with Brasso,' says George with a smile. 'A good cabin was a gleaming mass of metal, at least as beautifully kept as a cab on a locomotive.'

It was accepted practice that the telegraph lad would operate the levers while the signalman had his breakfast. This was all a bit unofficial, but it wasn't difficult, says George, because the signalman was always on hand if you got stuck and it didn't take long, anyway, to become familiar with the way the system worked.

'Mind you, there was a knack to pulling those levers – they weren't power-assisted or anything, so you had to put your weight behind them. Distant signals were more difficult simply *because* they were farther off – down below the cabin were the rods and linkages that led off up or down the track, and for a signal a good distance away you were moving a lot of metal, although counterbalancing weights were fitted to make things a little easier. Some points were particularly difficult: first you had to unlock them, then get clearance – that is, prove that nothing was on that bit of track – then you had to open the bar-point lock, a lock lever that kept the points where you wanted them. Only then could you go ahead.'

Signalboxes were almost like closed worlds with rules of their own and the signalman and his telegraph lad, if he had one, had to be self-sufficient. There was a stove for heating up tea and even meals, and there were chemical loos…

'The poor old telegraph lad had the job of emptying those too!' says George. 'What a terrible job that was, although at the Holloway box I was lucky because one of the platelayers used to do it, more often than not. But when I had to do it I had to walk across six or seven sets of tracks terrified I might slip and terrified I might have to move quick if a train came

along, and of course moving sharpish was very likely to make you drop the loo. I remember when Chitty Mason, a cattle-truck cleaner at Holloway sidings, was emptying this loo, and he tripped while crossing the tracks; of course the contents of the loo went everywhere – Dusty Day, the signalman I worked for at the time, could hardly operate the levers he was laughing so much.'

Signalboxes were held strictly to account in the old days; if there was an accident, however minor, the telegraph lad's entries were checked in the registration book, so everything had to be spot on. The big clock in the cabin was checked every day at 10am, and if it had to be corrected even by half a minute, a note to that effect had to be entered in the book. When a relief signalman came on he would rely heavily on the telegraph boy who usually knew a great deal more about the business of that particular box than the temporary signalman:

'I remember at Holloway South the relief signalman was George Gunn – he was known as Gun Gun for some reason – an enormous fellow who didn't like any of the drivers. The drivers all knew this, and to tease him they used to slow down as they passed the box and pretend to shoot him, a sort of reminder of his nickname. It used to infuriate George who would then report the drivers. Once, for no particular reason, he told me I'd been cheeky: "Get on your stool and stay on it for the rest of the shift," he said. So I sat there for a while, and then he went to the back of the box where the big old range provided heat and a place to cook his breakfast. All the signalmen cooked their breakfasts in the cabin in those days. He used to have half-a-dozen eggs, half-a-dozen pieces of bacon, sausages, fried bread – you wouldn't believe anyone could eat so much, he absolutely packed it away. Anyway, on this particular day I think he must have spent a bit longer than usual cooking because by the time he'd started eating, we were into a very busy time; in fact we were suddenly so busy that he asked me to move the points – but I told him I wouldn't because he'd told me to stay on my stool. I had the pleasure of watching him running back and forth between his enormous breakfast and the levers, and all the while he was cursing me. In the end he got so cross that he threw his breakfast, plate and everything, out of the window!'

By this time the war was in full swing and the main control offices for the railways were evacuated from London; for example the King's Cross control room went up to Knebworth in Hertfordshire where it remains to this day. At the Holloway box George and his signalman would frequently receive what was called a London Central Yellow warning if enemy bombers were known to be in the area during the day; a London Central Red meant the bombers were really close.

'Sometimes I wondered why they bothered to warn us,' says George, 'since there was nothing we could do. We just sat there like sitting targets and dimmed our lights a bit. It was mainly gas lights in those days so they were pretty dim anyway, and all the windows were blacked out with a hole left just big enough for the signalman to look out and peer up and down the line.

'In the back of the cabin at Holloway they fitted a steel shelter, actually inside the cabin. Old Dusty used to get nervy when there were bombers about, so he'd go into the shelter at the back of the box and tell me to get on with it. If bombs fell nearby I was supposed to dash into the steel box with him and sit on his lap – it was so small there was only room for the two of us that way. It always seemed funny to me, sitting there with this great big registration book open on my knees while Dusty held up an oil lamp so I could continue to fill the

George on his motorbike in the 1940s

book in. That metal box shelter was a complete waste of time, too – it was just a heavy steel box, so if the cabin had been hit it would have gone crashing down through the floor and we'd have been killed anyway. I suppose the idea was that it would at least protect us from flying glass.'

London at this time was definitely a scary place to be: all over the capital throughout the Blitz the German bombs could be heard going off, followed by the sound of anti-aircraft guns.

'Bombs often dropped near us,' says George, 'because the railways were a prime target. One night a massive bomb hit the ground right in front of our box, but by a miracle it just buried itself and failed to explode. If it had gone off some employees would have been killed, for sure.' As well as the constant risk of death at work, George had to cope with the very real danger of being killed at home. Like many Londoners, George has a fascinating tale of a narrow escape:

'It was 26 February 1941 – I can remember the exact date – and late that evening our next-door neighbour came round and asked us to join her. My dad had told my mum not to leave the house whatever happened because his theory was that if a bomb was going to get you, it would get you wherever you were, so you might as well stay in the house. So my mum said no and we stayed put. A short while later our neighbour came in again; she was upset, and asked us again to join her. I think she just wanted company. Anyway, Mum again refused, and she stuck to her guns until the neighbour became hysterical. Then at last we relented and trooped into next door. A short while later our house took a direct hit and there's no doubt at all that if we'd stayed put we'd have all been killed; as it was they had to dig us out! There was a lot of bombing in the Potters Bar area because there were three railway tunnels in the area, and the Germans knew they would cause huge disruption if they managed to damage any of them.

'We moved to my grandmother's after that, and her roof was then blown off in an air raid. My mum was getting a bit paranoid by now – she thought the Germans were really after her, so she went to Devon to her mum's and dad's house, and would you believe it, she was bombed out there, too!'

As the war went on, George was promoted to relief telegraph boy; he also started doing night duties. Despite the difficult hours and long journeys, the job of relief telegraph boy was considered prestigious:

'In 1943, when I was seventeen, two of us were selected to train as signalmen. I knew a lot already from my days as a telegraph lad, but to be a full signalman you had to know a hell of a lot more, as I quickly discovered when I was sent to the signals training school at

Hatfield.' This school was established in a former royal waiting room on one of the platforms, and the story of how it came to be there provides an interesting glimpse of the relationship between railways and royalty in former times.

Queen Victoria had often visited Hatfield, because it is the nearest station to Hatfield House, home of the Cecils. In order to accommodate the Queen, the platforms at Hatfield were built staggered – in other words, they are built in such a way that they do not face each other across the tracks in the normal way. This meant that when the royal train stopped at the station, there was no chance that another train could stop opposite the royal train, and so there was no risk of the Queen being ogled by her subjects. The Hatfield royal waiting room was kept in perfect order, but in fact it was never used – until 1943 when the national emergency persuaded officials that they'd better make some use of it. And so it became a signals school for young men like George.

'When my mate and I turned up at Hatfield we found we were joined by two trainee tele-graph girls and three women training as guards; they were the first women ever to be trained in those jobs. Our training lasted three weeks; we were given a test to see if we knew the rules and regulations, and then we were off to our own signalboxes. I was sent to Crews Hill on the Hertford Loop. Every frame – that's the bit in the box that the levers are in – is dif-ferent, so you had to be trained for the specific box you were going to work in. At Crews Hill it was what was called a porter signalman's job: in other words, it was a tiny station where you did a bit of everything, signals, booking clerk, stationmaster, porter. In fact there wasn't much signal work to be done, and you only really opened up the cabin to shorten the block or to perform shunting duties. The more block sections you had, the more trains there were, because there was one train to a block. The idea was that so long as you knew there could only ever be one train in a block section, you knew the trains were being kept safely apart. But you always had to keep your eyes and ears open for things that weren't quite right – as a train went by you'd always look at the back of it, for example, to make sure its tail lamp was there: if it wasn't, it meant that half the train had got lost somewhere! That really did happen in the old days when wagons were loose coupled.

'I had a bit of help at Crews Hill in the shape of a lad porter who had better remain nameless, but for the sake of the story let's call him Monty. All I can say is, he was a real no-gooder; he was always late and he was always up to something. He was supposed to light the station's oil lamps as well as the oil lamps in the signalbox when he arrived, so if he was late it was a real nuisance. One day I was up in the box when a young lad walked up to me and said: "I've come for the oil. Is Monty about?"

George, porter-signalman at Crews Hill

"No," I replied in complete bafflement.

"I've got the can," he said and proceeded to wave it under my nose.

"What?" I said.

"Don't you know the dodge here?" came the reply.

'Well, it turned out that this chap had been buying our lamp oil from Monty at 6d a go. I put a stop to it immediately.'

Crews Hill was situated in the middle of a large area of nurseries so much of the freight traffic was associated with this industry, and one of George's most delightful stories arose as a result of this connection:

'One morning the stationmaster, who looked after three stations including Crews Hill, turned up early. He asked me to stay behind and told me that the best kept station competition was to be judged in the area that day and he wanted to win the prize. There was £2 in it for the stationmaster, 10s for me and my mate Joe Ward, five bob for the lad porter and a little something for the booking clerks; the total prize was a fiver.

'Crews Hill had plenty of flowerbeds so we set about re-whitening the edges of these, and then the stationmaster sent us down to the nearest nursery, which backed on to the station, to get some plants that were in flower and would therefore look really good. We raced off with several big barrows, came back with the plants and buried them in the soil complete with their pots! Within a couple of hours the whole station was transformed – it looked absolutely beautiful. A little later the special train arrived with the district superintendent

aboard. Our stationmaster immediately began sucking up to him like mad – "Would you care for a piece of this cake? My wife made it this morning," and suchlike. Anyway, the superintendent was impressed and said so. He got back on the train, having said we were in the running for the prize, and off he went. As soon as he was out of sight, the stationmaster shouted to us to get the barrows, dig up the plants, still in their pots, and take them straight back to the nursery! Disgraceful really, but we won first prize.

'This particular stationmaster used to take vegetables and fruit from the owner of one nursery if he failed to take delivery of his coal within a specified time; he should have been fined, really, but the stationmaster was happy to take grub in lieu! When the circus trains used to stop at High Barnet this same stationmaster – then a lad, but his dad was stationmaster – used to charge the local kids a penny to watch the elephants being exercised; that's how he got his nickname, Jumbo!'

Like most railwaymen, George continued to move around a great deal as he changed jobs. After two years at Crews Hill he went to Cuffley Station, then on to Palmers Green, then Enfield, all posts in the North London/Hertfordshire area. He got his first job on the main line in Hornsey Number One signalbox:

'Hornsey was a bit scary at first because you were dealing with expresses. I'll never forget the first day I spent in the box on my own – it was a hell of a responsibility because you didn't get any second chances; what you did had to be spot on, or there could be a disaster. I spent three weeks in that box being trained; it was a bit like the system with drivers where they had to know the road, in other words the route, before they were allowed to drive the engine over it. With signals you had to know your box before they left you to get on with it. On the day you were finally to be tested the district inspector would come along, then the regular signalman would step back and say to you, "All right lad, get on with it!" The two of them then watched to see if you made any mistakes.

'Each track had a bell telling you a train was coming and a bell telling you the train was going away, and there were eight bells at Hornsey, covering four sets of tracks. The bells were on a shelf above you and each one had a different tone, so you had to know which tone was which in order to answer. If you got the wrong bell, the man who'd sent you the signal would signal back with a sarcastic ring. I know it's hard to imagine, but you really could ring the bell sarcastically; if I made a mistake and replied to the wrong signalbox when a bell rang, the returning signal would instantly make me aware that the other man was saying, "Come on you nit-wit, get it right!" You didn't want to let yourself down in front of people, so you very quickly got to know the sound of each bell!'

At peak periods George found that he was dashing around pulling levers for all he was worth, but there were slacker periods when he could heat up something to eat on the range at the back of the box. All signalmen cooked, and many would take the ingredients for a complete roast dinner if they were working on a Sunday. 'I remember one old boy used to nip out of the box, run across to a nearby allotment and help himself to some onions which he then added to his meal,' says George with a grin.

After Hornsey, George moved to Wood Green, to a box that overlooked the racecourse at Alexandra Palace: 'That was great, because from my box I had a better view of the horses than anyone anywhere on the track itself. I'd often look out the window, too, and see my father, who was a guard, waving to me as his train went past, and all the drivers waved so you never felt too lonely. You could also telephone your mates in signalboxes up and down the line.'

A typical LNER ballast train at Harrow-on-the-Hill; the down main line south of the station was being relaid with flat-bottomed rail (Milepost)

A signalman who worked on what was known as a continuous cabin had to work for twenty days before he was allowed a day off, and this would include two twelve-hour Sunday shifts. Shifts were either 6pm–6am or 6am–6pm, so the hours were long. When the union negotiated a reduction in the hours from forty-eight a week to forty-six, more staff were needed to cover for the rest-day relief.

The contingency that all railwaymen dreaded in the pre-electronic age was bad weather, particularly fog, but for the signalman there were also the practical difficulties associated with relatively primitive equipment: 'If a signal lamp went out you could be in trouble,' remembers George. 'When they were trimmed and lit – they were all oil – they were supposed to last eight days, but through human error, a badly trimmed wick or whatever,

perhaps high winds, they might go out. This was particularly dangerous if a light went out on the gantry above the lines and the signalman might have to re-light it. Those rickety old gantries high above the rails were bloody awful places to be, I can tell you, and in bad weather (when you were most likely to have to go up there) they could be terrifying. I remember going up to light a lamp when there was a terrific gale blowing and it was pitch black. I didn't think I'd ever get down, and when I did, I hardly knew where I was. It was pitch black that night.

'Fog was the biggest killer of all because fogs then, the old pea-soupers, would reduce visibility to a few feet. Everything slowed down and we'd bring the fog signalmen on.'

George continued as a signalman until 1955, but his obvious abilities, combined with the shortage of men in the years following the end of hostilities, meant he was promoted to assistant controller.

'This was at Knebworth and I was eventually responsible for everything from King's Cross to Barkston in Lincolnshire. I had to know every inch of those 108 miles as well as the sections of loop line. A class five assistant controller, which was where I started, was at the bottom of the pile; you had to do all the record keeping, check that all the trains were running on time, stoke the fire in the office and make the tea for all the controllers.' By starting at the bottom as an assistant controller George lost £3 a week in wages, but the prospects were good. After four months he went back into the signal grade (his assistant controller job was as a summer relief only). Soon after that he was sent to Peterborough which, in the 1950s, was incredibly busy.

'The first thing I remember about that job was that I was put in charge of giving the drivers salt tablets! These were regulation issue because driving was such warm work, and losing too much salt through sweating is very bad for you. I also had to go to the drivers' barracks in the town and wake them up in the morning. I'd walk along in the dark with a list of names in my hand tapping on various windows with a long pole.'

By 1955 George was working as a full-time assistant controller, and by the 1960s he'd taken over as assistant stationmaster at King's Cross. 'I'd known I wanted that job years earlier when the assistant stationmaster at King's Cross had said to me, "Where's your hat?" I told him I didn't have one – I was a signalman at the time, and signalmen never did, but he obviously had no idea. Anyway he sent me home, so off I went. But halfway along the platform he called me back and told me to go to the stores and get something for my head. I went, picked up the first hat that came to hand, got a pen and some ink and scrubbed out the words "Ticket Collector" which were printed on the front of it. That assistant stationmaster then asked me what my ambition was, so I said I wanted to be an assistant stationmaster like him so I could boss people about the way he did. "Get out, you cheeky devil!" he replied. I did nearly twenty years as an assistant stationmaster, and for much of that time I was acting stationmaster. It was a great job.'

Signalboxes all disappeared in the late 1970s and early 1980s, and these days trains are all monitored and controlled electronically; but George wouldn't have missed a minute of his early years: 'I'm glad I had my time working the old levers. The men I worked with both then and later on were a great bunch, and there were some very funny moments. I remember particularly Chitty Mason who kept the platforms tidy at King's Cross. One day Princess Margaret had just arrived and was about to get off her train when Chitty spotted a poodle using the red carpet in an unmentionable fashion outside her carriage. Quick as a flash he leapt over, picked up the poodle dropping and put it in his pocket. He walked calmly over to me and simply said, "That was a near miss, guv!"

'Perhaps the funniest thing in all my forty-three years' service was my meeting with Anthony Barber when he was Chancellor of the Exchequer. He borrowed two bob from me, and would you believe it – some flippin' chancellor – he never paid it back!'

GENTLEMEN AT THE TOP!

RICHARD HARDY
Shedmaster on the London &
North Eastern Railway

Richard Hardy is a most unusual railwayman. A former public schoolboy, he began his career in 1941 as an apprentice engineer making nuts and bolts, and ended up at the Railways Board. Starting almost at the bottom he worked his way almost to the top, and what began as the stirrings of a passion at the age of four ended in an enthusiasm that took him through forty-two years of practical experience with steam, diesel and electric traction. He remembers: 'I was given a clockwork engine when I was four, and then I was taken to the station at Leatherhead in Surrey by my mother. This would have been in 1927.'

The moment of truth came in 1929, however, when he was given a copy of the January edition of the *Railway Magazine*: 'That was it,' he says with a gleam in his eye. 'I didn't understand much of it, but by and by that monthly magazine gave me a wonderful grounding for life on the railway.'

Although he was born in Leatherhead, Surrey, the son of a retired tea-planter, Richard and his family had moved to Amersham in Buckinghamshire by the time he was ten. An only child, but very happy, he was to spend long hours on Amersham station platform watching the trains roar by. But he never took their numbers because he didn't want simply to record the existence of the great engines, but to understand how they worked: 'The great Central engines, passing through Amersham, really hooked me,' he says. 'I was on the platform every day of the holidays when I came home from school at Marlborough. I got to know all the railway staff, who were incredibly friendly. Eventually the footplate men knew me, too, and I was given trips to Rickmansworth and Wendover. Can you imagine that now? Not likely!'

Now seventy-five, Richard lives in a house on the edge of Amersham with his wife Gwenda; he's lived here for more than twenty years: 'The longest I've been anywhere,' he says with a grin – like many railwaymen, he spent much of his career working in different parts of the country. He is still full of the memory of his early enthusiasm:

'My interest simply grew and grew,' he says, 'and everything seemed to conspire to make me more interested. For example, in 1931 I had a holiday at Mexborough in Yorkshire with my governess, when I would have been about seven. As luck would have it, my governess's father was a coal merchant and her uncle chief clerk at Doncaster Locomotive sheds. Apart from helping deliver coal, which we collected at the railway yard and which I enjoyed enormously, I spent a day of that holiday at the huge engine shed at Mexborough, another at Doncaster Carr Loco, where I would be working as an apprentice thirteen years later, a day at York at the railway museum, and endless hours on Mexborough station.

'I can also remember my first trip on the footplate, in 1933. I was at school at Seaford in Sussex and my parents were taking me to Brighton by train one Sunday. We had to change at Lewes, and when our train ran in from Tonbridge, we went up to look at the engine. I must have stood there looking up at the driver with my mouth open. Just imagine my surprise when he asked me if I wanted to climb up and go to Falmer with him. I was in heaven, I can tell you, and he took me on to London Road, Brighton where I was put back in the train. I can still remember the engine, a Sterling F1 built for the South Eastern Railway in about 1892. Among southern enginemen they were known affectionately as Flying Bedsteads.'

Determined on a railway career, Richard left Marlborough at the age of seventeen. His reasons were partly financial – 'my mother couldn't really afford it after my father died' – but he was pleased to be starting work in the industry that had so captivated him: 'I went straight into a job as an apprentice at Doncaster, and I can remember the exact date – it was 17 January 1941. An older friend at school had gone to the LMS and I thought rather vaguely that I ought to follow him; but my heart was in the LNER, and when I saw Col Pullein-Thompson, the careers adviser, he went straight to the point: "Go on the LNER boy! Gentlemen at the top!"'

Richard began his life on the railways making motion pins and bolts on a lathe, but from his earliest days he was interested in everything that was happening, and enjoyed the company of his workmates, young and old. He did his practical work on the lathe during the day, and was expected to do his theory at home at night.

'Oh, you were expected to do as you were told, and long hours and strict conditions were the norm. You were only paid when you came to work, for I wasn't salaried in those days and

Amersham station in the summer of 1936 (H. C. Casserley)

being late on duty was a serious matter. During my apprenticeship I was late once. I was going to work on my bike at 3am one moonlit Sunday morning when a policeman stopped me for not having a light – I was ten minutes late for work, lost half an hour's pay and was fined 10s.'

Richard's public school accent must have sounded incongruous among the other apprentices, but few tricks were played on him by the older boys and indeed he has fond memories of his contemporaries' kindnesses. When his one pair of boots hurt his feet, for example, someone suggested he wear clogs which were still popular in the north in those days.

'They cost 8s 6d the pair, and only one clothing coupon,' remembers Richard, 'but they were very comfortable and once saved me from serious injury to my foot when I'd got caught between the fallplate and the tender end of a GN Atlantic on a sharp curve in York yard. The thick wooden sole of the clog took the squeeze, not my foot, which would have been crushed if I'd been wearing ordinary boots. When my mother came to visit me once she was so taken by the clogs that she bought herself a fancy-coloured lady's pair!'

Richard started work as what was then known as a premium apprentice, which meant his mother had to pay a premium of £50 to get him in. 'I believe I was the last premium apprentice on the LNER until after the war, and those that followed me had the same training but without the premium. I have always believed that an engineering apprenticeship is an education in engineering *and* in human relationships. In those days it was all very autocratic, but as I moved through the various engineering departments I discovered that the men I worked with never asked me to work harder than they were prepared and able to work themselves.'

Lifelong friendships were established in those early days, and Richard is still in close touch with Stan Hodgson, who was a fireman when Richard first met him one night in May 1941. At Wakefield, the extrovert Stan invited Richard, a scruffy seventeen-year-old, onto the engine of the London Mail. At Doncaster and before returning to Leeds at two in the morning, the driver, Bob Foster, and Stan took Richard in hand to explain to him the essentials of their job: 'You'll be a boss one day and you'll have to know our job inside out, else you'll be neither use nor ornament; so come and see us every evening that you get the chance and we'll put you through it.'

'After that I never looked back, and the West Riding men in particular, many of whom were in their late fifties and early sixties, went to endless trouble to teach me their job in all its complexity; but above all, I was learning about railwaymen. They had nothing to gain by doing this and I shall never forget their kindness, for in my Doncaster years I covered about 60,000 miles on the footplate, most of it in my spare time and outside my official training.'

By the end of 1943 Richard had finished his training in the plant works and was transferred to the running shed; here, in the rough and dirty life of maintaining engines in steam to meet the never-ending demands of wartime traffic, he was in his element. He worked with a number of different fitters, and he was also a member of a breakdown gang which, manning a big forty-five-ton crane, was called out to all derailments of engines, carriages and wagons in a wide area. He enjoyed this work immensely and was a sort of mascot to the members of the gang, all in their forties and fifties, and to the foreman, a Mr Palmer, who loved to take the mickey out of him. Apart from working on breakdowns, Richard went on lifting jobs: putting in a new turntable at Lincoln for example, and loading a midget submarine on a rail wagon in the early hours in absolute secrecy.

'It is important to remember the difference between the plant works which was a factory, and the running shed,' he says. 'In the plant works, the discipline was pretty rigid, planning was essential, and production and output were the ever-present targets. At first sight, the running shed life, with its endless movement of engines in steam, its drivers and firemen and its artisans, might have seemed to offer greater freedom, and at times, things could be quiet for an hour; but then the scene would change, and skilled men, fitters and boilermakers could rise to amazing heights of endeavour to keep the traffic moving, for the enemy at the shed was the timetable, the clock and the fearful demands of the wartime railway.'

Working conditions were very rough: no heating in the shed, and no way to wash up except in a bucket of paraffin; but Richard enjoyed it all and the great camaraderie. Then in November 1944 he left the running shed for the drawing office where he spent his last nine months at Doncaster. 'I was a poor affair at the drawing board,' he says, 'although the draughtsmen themselves were able engineers and very good company. I remember designing

the lubricator drive for Great Northern, the rebuilt A1, and thinking that I had made a nice job of it; but when it came to be assembled on the engine, oh dear, what a story! I was *not* popular! Nevertheless I learned a great deal that was useful to me in later life – though I knew perfectly well that, above all, I wanted to make my career in the rough and tumble of the running department.'

In June 1945 Richard was interviewed by the locomotive running superintendent, L. P. Parker – a legendary figure among railwaymen – and two months later was sent, as a progressman, to Stratford in East London. At that time Stratford was the biggest running shed in the world, housing over 500 engines with thousands of men:

'Nothing else like it, and all ghosts now,' says Richard. 'L. P. Parker was respected and feared, and he drove us young men – "my young men" as he called us – mercilessly; but when we had proved ourselves, he gave us the sort of responsibility no other superintendent would have considered giving to men of our age.

'I was working at his headquarters at Liverpool Street when I got married in 1949. After our honeymoon I returned to work, and he sent for me. "Hardy," he said, "I have a pleasant surprise for your wife: I am sending you to Cambridge for a few weeks," which meant lodgings, working all hours, seven days a week and no going home at the weekend. There was no argument with L. P. – but then he wanted his young men to get to the top, and we learned the hard way.'

By January 1946 Richard was working under the shedmaster at King's Lynn, and this life of ever-changing locations – with two-, three- and four-year stints in widely different parts of the country – was to continue almost until he retired.

'On my arrival at King's Lynn, on a very cold, dark day, Ted Shaw, the shedmaster, a tough Mancunian who didn't think much of younger men, asked me if I took snuff; so I tried it, and of course it made me sneeze. Ted was sardonically amused and told me I was "nowt but a bloody kid". Far worse things had been said to me at Marlborough, however, so I didn't mind in the least – and anyway I had a great admiration for Ted. He had me doing the daily enginemen's rosters and the engine list, as well as seeing to repairs and other work in the shed, coaling, boiler washing and cleaning of engines. The rostering was a minefield, particularly when upgrading passed firemen to drivers and getting the right men in the right place. The staff watched every move, and I got hell if I made a mistake – "You're wasting the company money," they used to say. But I used the principles that Ted Shaw drilled into me to solve many a roster dispute in later life.

'After a few months he considered that I could just about manage without him, so he then spent a fair amount of time in the East Anglian pub – he liked his beer, I can tell you. When he went on leave I took his place, and when you take charge, you really begin to learn.'

Employment conditions were far harsher in the 1940s, and at Richard's level few enjoyed sick pay or were part of the pension scheme: 'Few people were salaried in those days,' he recalls, 'so men struggled into work if they were ill, where these days some would stay at home. You were paid for being there, and got nothing if you failed to come in. There were no salaries for drivers, guards, platelayers, firemen or supernumerary firemen – in fact hardly anyone got a salary.' But despite these disadvantages, engine driving and working on the railway were seen as glamorous jobs. Richard remembers that at many stations where the trains stopped for long enough people would gather round the engine and talk to the driver and fireman.

'Now, of course, the driver is boxed in and the job doesn't have that special atmosphere about it, although, of course, the responsibility is the same with all those passengers relying on him.'

It took Richard a total of eight years to become a shedmaster. He was finally given his own shed at Woodford on the Great Central, where he had to manage 280 men and 50 engines, a tall order for a young man; but it was a job he loved: 'At Woodford, our engine-men worked to Marylebone, Nottingham, Banbury and Sheffield with passenger trains, but our shed was largely freight, to Banbury, Neasden, and the night express freight trains from Marylebone to Sheffield and Manchester. Freight work was considerable in those days because there were no motorways and the massive container lorries of the modern world simply didn't exist. If you had freight to move you had to use the railways.' This meant, of course, that men like Richard laboured under great responsibility.

Richard's wife had their first child in 1950 and at almost the same time he was sent to Ipswich. Again there was that sense that for the railwayman the job had to come first: 'I was very happy at Woodford and my district locomotive superintendent at Nottingham tried to get Mr Parker to send somebody else; but L. P. simply replied, "If Hardy doesn't go to Ipswich, he will not go anywhere for a very long time!"

'Trying to find somewhere to live on £420 a year wasn't easy; we rented a thatched cottage near Woodford – a lovely little place, but no running water, and a hand-pump – though at Ipswich, British Railways had bought a small house for the shedmaster.'

At Ipswich the shed dated back to 1846, and working conditions were cramped; the men had to coal the tenders by hand because there was no mechanical coaling plant, and only eleven engines could be under cover at any one time out of a total of ninety-one. 'There were about 450 men at the shed,' says Richard; 'some of the most conscientious men I have ever worked with. Working conditions were a challenge, but the standard of maintenance and pride in the job was unforgettable. I have always kept in touch with the Ipswich men through their ASLEF retired drivers' gatherings, to which I am still invited from time to time.

'We had some very old engines dating back to the 1890s; they were simple and straightforward and no trouble to anybody. Our passenger engines were B1s, B17s and the famous GE B12s. The B1s (or Bongos as they were known) and the B12s had their own regular crews. There were two sets of men to an engine, and this generated tremendous rivalry as to whose was the best and most highly polished, the cab shining like a jeweller's shop.'

After a little over two years at Ipswich, Richard found himself posted to Stewart's Lane, Battersea, in South London. This was very different from Ipswich. Here, on the Southern Region, punctuality was a religion: 'Our drivers were accountable for every minute lost, and I was accountable to my chief,' says Richard. 'If a driver lost two minutes from Victoria to Herne Hill after a tough time climbing the grade out of Victoria, he would no doubt regain it by Tonbridge, but the two minutes went down against Stewart's Lane.

'There were two punctuality leagues, and your position in them was judged according to minutes lost per thousand miles run. We were always well up the first division, but never at the top because of the complexity of the services our men handled. It was a splendid discipline, although administratively it cost a lot of money, especially as any time loss which was disputed had to be settled, and any delays were pursued so that there would be no repetition by those responsible – which usually included the chap in charge, and rightly so! Woodford and Ipswich were positively gentlemanly compared with our tough, uncompromising Battersea boys!

'Of all the wonderful jobs I had, Stewart's Lane brought me nearest to the real running of the railway. Some 750 South London boys, most of them outspoken and critical of management, would nevertheless rise to the occasion to meet the demands of the summer service year after year. It was a remarkable job, hard work, seven days a week, and only a fortnight's holiday a year.

'When I needed a break I would go down to Dover on the engine of the *Golden Arrow*, maybe do the driving on the down and the firing on the up road, and that would put me right again. At

Fred Brown,
one of Richard's drivers at Stewart's Lane,
Battersea – 'a marvellous cockney'

Stewart's Lane, one had to be the guvn'r: if you were easy, you were finished because the Cockneys had no respect for an easy boss. You had to be fair and straight, so we had our battles – but they were good-hearted battles, with no grudges held. I still see some of the younger men of those days, including Teddy Champion, Reg Coote and Alf Pink. We used to row, and now we laugh about it, at a gathering each year near Victoria to which they invite me. I wouldn't miss it for anything!'

Having returned to Stratford as assistant district locomotive superintendent in January 1955, Richard was promoted to take charge of the district four years later. 'That meant that I was in overall charge of several sheds, including Stratford, and some three thousand men,' he recalls. This job put him in charge of the changeover from steam to diesel traction.

'It was as much a human revolution as a machine revolution,' he says now. 'Everybody's way of life was changed in four short years. It always amazed me how well the older men took to this dramatic change. No longer did drivers and firemen actually generate the engine's power, in a private world of their own and by the sweat of their brow, a challenge that made the steam men unique: now they worked in cleanliness and comfort. In the steam shed at Stratford on a warm Sunday evening, the conditions, with fires being lit and the place full of acrid smoke, were intolerable and dangerous, for men could barely see their hands in front of their faces. But when the diesel depot was opened, our men worked in conditions of order and cleanliness they had never imagined could exist.'

Although impressed by the professionalism of virtually all the men he worked with,

Richard has a special fondness for the running shed artisans: 'These were the men who kept the engines going. The best were craftsmen, but at the same time, they had to be masters of expediency whether with steam or the new diesel locomotives. One sometimes forgets that we converted boilermakers to electricians and they took the change in their stride.'

One of the highlights of Richard's career came when he was asked to show the Queen round the depot at Stratford. He remembers being impressed by how well she'd been briefed: 'She asked all the right questions. For example, I introduced her to a driver who instructed on diesels, and she asked him straightaway if he preferred steam to diesel. "The diesel is clean and interesting ma'am," he said, "but it's nothing like my Old John Bunyan."

'That said it all for most of the enginemen, though the artisans preferred the challenges of the new traction, and the working conditions. Again, the footplate staff missed the camaraderie, the companionship, the challenges of steam, the personal contact with the public and with thousands of would-be young railwaymen – but the new forms of traction transformed the railway and there can be no going back. However, it does make you realise what miracles of service, speed and efficiency were achieved in the past.'

This sense of the difficulties associated with engines seems to have become more acute in Richard as the steam era receded: 'Imagine what it was like for a sixteen-year-old boy to

'…tender first running in freezing fog'

be confronted, on a scorching Sunday afternoon, with the task of cleaning the fire of a King Arthur that had arrived back at the shed with a firebox full of fire and clinker. Using the long, nine-foot fire irons, the youngster had to break up the great mass of solid clinker and draw it out on a heavy, long-handled, red-hot clinker shovel. It was a hell of a job, and it's no wonder many boys didn't have the stomach for the work, and the awkward hours. Come to that, tender first running in freezing fog could be pretty rough, too – frozen one side and roasted the other!'

But like all railwaymen who worked on steam, Richard is proud of the tremendous skills involved in keeping the locomotives in good running order, despite the pressures of time and money: 'You had to know exactly what you were doing, while keeping an eye on half-a-dozen things at once. It was like juggling with plates – no sooner had you sorted out one problem, than another arose which was more urgent than the first. And carelessness had to be dealt with severely, because self-discipline was part of our way of life. For example, a driver and fireman could be suspended or removed from the footplate if they allowed the water level to fall seriously low in the boiler so that the lead plug, a safety measure in the firebox, melted.'

At Stratford, as assistant district loco supervisor, Richard was greatly concerned with the chronic shortage of engines throughout the district; such were the demands on maintenance

Richard (right) with Joe Oglesby from Sheffield

that the shift foremen were having engines 'stopped' for boiler washout in the evening, washed out with cold water by the night shift, then boxed up, lit up and fired by 1am ready for early morning work.

'To wash out a blazing hot boiler with cold water is asking for trouble, but the engines were needed and the staff co-operated to get the job done. The water spaces were not cleaned out, and the examinations by the boilermakers were cursory until one day, through a build-up of dirt, some firebox stays broke and bulged under full steam pressure on an L1 working a passenger train.'

Overnight, Richard drew up instructions so that every man involved throughout the district knew what he had to do; he discussed this fully with all concerned, and supported the boiler examiners on whom so much depended. 'Initially this was highly unpopular at Stratford, but we won the day and the condition of the engines improved which made life less fraught for the shift foremen.'

Richard's diligence and devotion to railway transport – he never even considered changing careers – finally paid off when he was promoted to a job at the Railways Board. 'I say *at* because I don't mean *on* the board,' he says carefully. 'There is a considerable difference! I came to BR headquarters via King's Cross where I became divisional manager in 1964, after a spell at Lincoln and then at Liverpool from 1968 to the end of 1973. The last thing I wanted to do was to leave Liverpool, having been a front-line man all my working life, but I was eventually made responsible for the career development of all engineers in every department of BR, dealing with the youngest sponsored student at university one moment, or the choice and appointment of a head of department the next. I retired at the end of 1982 after all but forty-two years. My first week's wage packet was 16s 2d [81p]. I had better not tell you what I was paid at the end – not much by today's standards! But I never really thought of doing anything else; like all railwaymen, I loved the job even in the days when I washed my hands in paraffin, got on my bike still in my overalls and, almost exhausted, cycled back to my digs late at night. No one had cars in those wartime days, and I remember Doncaster was swarming with men and women on bikes – and many were railway workers.'

Once in those very early years Richard remembers working ninety-eight hours one week in very hard weather with the Doncaster breakdown gang; this earned him his first £5 note. 'I had never seen one, and nor had many other men in overalls,' he recalls with a chuckle. 'I knew that shopkeepers would look askance at a boy in overalls offering one of those great white £5 notes in Doncaster, but in the end, I got a friend to change it.'

In his shedmaster days Richard was responsible for three grades: the footplate staff – drivers and firemen; the artisans – boilermakers, fitters and other craftsmen; and what were called the shed conciliation grades. 'I still don't know the origin of that unusual name,' he says, 'but the conciliation men ranged from timekeepers, storesmen, toolmen and boiler washers to tube cleaners and shed labourers.

'Many of the men with whom I worked had left school at twelve or thirteen and had little formal education. Yet year after year, day and night, and in fog or snow, drivers and firemen – unlettered men, trained only by experience – shouldered responsibility for the lives of thousands. It was a way of life; but it could come to an end all too suddenly because the medical requirements were stringent, and failing eyesight, or colour blindness, or heart trouble, or loss of confidence meant removal from the footplate into the conciliation grades, a bitter disappointment with serious financial implications. It was very hard, and I have seen it happen all too often.'

Despite the relative harshness of his earliest days on the railway, Richard has only happy memories of the 1940s: 'For me as a youngster it was marvellous. Men, some old enough to be my grandfather, took me in hand and taught me all they knew, giving me experience that stood me in good stead for the rest of my railway life. I treasure the large album of photographs I took with my little Box Brownie of the men I worked with in those days – every picture prompts a memory of an adventure, of special engines and friends, most of whom have long since died.

'I suppose my favourite engines were the GN Atlantics; they were rough and uncomfortable,

'I suppose my favourite engines were GN Atlantics…'

61

Richard (left) with driver Ted Hailstone at Ardsley in Yorkshire

but magnificent uphill and they would always race across the level and with plenty of steam to spare. I remember once flying down Beeston Bank towards Leeds on an Atlantic. When we took the curve through Beeston Station at over sixty miles an hour we thought – or at least I did! – that our last hour had come. But the driver I was with, Bill Denman of Leeds, knew what he was about.

'Another driver I remember well was Bob Foster with whom I rode on the famous 4472 *Flying Scotsman*. With its low pressure boiler it wasn't one of the best, but it was an education to see Bob making small, delicate alterations to the valve travel to suit the road, according to whether it was level, uphill or down. Another fine driver was Alf Cartwright – he was a big man, slow-moving and with a great sense of humour. He once stopped by mistake at a station and was given an absolute roasting by the stationmaster. Calm as you like he replied: "We'd better go, then. It's a long time since we saw you so we stopped to see how you were going on." Like many drivers in the West Riding who worked with firemen in their forties, Alf did his share of the firing while his mate took hold.

'I once fired a Valour for Alf from Wakefield to Grantham and I remember the quiet, unhurried way he went about his business, making life easy for me. On another journey, this time from Wakefield to Bradford with a chap called George Stoyles, I was given a literary lecture – George knew everything there was to know about the Brontë sisters, and as we roared along he lectured me on *Wuthering Heights*!

'Perhaps my greatest mentor was Ted Hailstone, who my mother thought had the look and presence of a bishop. The first time we met, he told me that he would make a fireman of me and then a driver. Looking back, I am amazed at the opportunities he gave me. He also told me what he expected of a shedmaster, or a superintendent. He was always interested in my career, and each time I gained promotion in later years he expected me to let him know, whereupon I would receive a reply finishing, "Yours ever forward".

'He was a very hard taskmaster who inspired either immense admiration or loathing in those who worked with him. He came from a railway family in Manchester and was a stickler for self-discipline and tidiness. When you saw him in action, either driving or firing, you knew that here was a man who had mastered the engineman's profession. My firing had to be precise, he expected full steam pressure where it was needed, and the minimum of smoke and waste of steam. If I failed to sweep up after every firing, he would stand and shuffle his clogs until I did so; many West Riding men wore clogs in those days. In later years he moved from Bradford to King's Cross and I fired for him, for old time's sake, to Leeds and back on his own A4 Pacific *Silver Link* just before he retired in 1956. He was a good friend.

'I learned with Ted the utter importance of concentration: never to let the mind wander, and never, never to talk when running into a station, or when the signals were at caution or at danger, or up to a speed restriction. To pass a signal at danger was a crime – and still is, I am sure. I was to experience that, too, so I know the awful feeling.

'On one occasion I was firing to a marvellous character, Harold Binder, on an N5 5901, from Bradford to Halifax. A few minutes before going I got the camera out and took a photograph of Harold and his mate on the front gangway. But when we returned, I realised that I had left the injector at work and had overfilled the boiler. We started away, but when we got on the 1 in 45 and Harold opened the regulator wide, 5901 'caught the water' and we roared up the grade to St Dunstans, water pouring from the chimney and cylinder cocks, not much more than walking pace. I had to struggle all the way to Queensbury – but we kept time and Harold's greatly embellished rebuke always makes me laugh. But it was yet another lesson learned.'

Such is Richard's enthusiasm that it is difficult to keep up with the rich flow of stories he can conjure from the past. As well as stories of firemen and drivers he remembers incidents from all areas of steam-working, including a fascinating meeting early in his career with his chief mechanical engineer Edward Thompson.

'I had been interviewed by Mr Thompson when I left school and he had taken an interest in my progress. Early in 1942, in the dark at Wakefield, he spotted me getting off an engine and asked me what I was doing so late on a Saturday evening. The fact that I was learning to fire pleased him greatly, even though it was highly unofficial! When the train for Doncaster ran in, he beckoned me to follow, sat me down in a compartment and then told me about his plans for building new locomotives: the B1, the L1, his Pacifics, rebuilt K1s, B17s and, of course, the splendid 04 rebuild, to become the even better O1. Not all his engines were to be perfect, but most were splendid jobs. He aimed to reduce the number of classes, to ease the lot of the running sheds by simplification and standardisation and, given the appalling wartime shortages of material, his short reign of five-and-a-half years was memorable.

'That night at Doncaster when he bade me goodnight he lifted his hat to me, a scruffy eighteen-year-old. Whereas some will always denigrate Thompson and his work, I shall never forget him: he sent me to Leslie Parker, and he knew he was sending me to the most outstanding manager of young men on the LNER. And for that I shall always be grateful.'

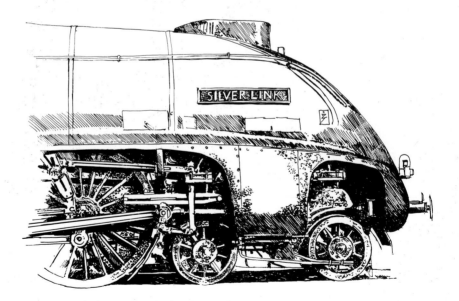

BRITAIN'S OLDEST RAILWAYMAN

VINSUN GULLIVER

*Driver on the London Midland & Scottish
and the London & North Eastern Railways*

At the time of writing Vinsun Gulliver is 109 and the oldest man in Britain. He is also an extraordinary survivor, for he is probably the only man left alive in Britain who has first-hand knowledge of what was, when he started work in 1907, effectively still a Victorian railway system. He caught the end of the great days of steam; the days, long before the motor car, when the railway was undisputed king.

Born in Upton, Warwickshire, in 1889 Vinsun started work at the station there cleaning engines on 3 September 1907. His memory of those far-off days is still vivid, despite the passing of more than eight decades: 'I can remember the smell of the engines, the smell of the oil and the long hours – well, they were long by today's standards, anyway.'

But in those days when you started at the bottom as Vinsun did, your job might include all sorts of tasks; in fact, as he explains, you did whatever you were asked to do, from making tea for the stationmaster to running errands: 'Yes, I carried out all sorts of tasks, and I supplemented my income by shovelling coal – as you can probably imagine, there was a lot of that to be done.'

Despite his great age, Vinsun is still an enormously animated character, and when it comes to distant memories his mind is still able to conjure up a magical picture of the past. He makes light of many of the more irritating afflictions of great age. 'I am really rather deaf,' he says mischievously, 'so you must bellow into my good ear!'

In other respects he is quite fit, and although he has been in a nursing home in Altrincham just outside Manchester for many years there is no sense that he has given up on life. The nurse who looks after him says that he announces regularly that he has had enough and has decided to die, but the mood quickly passes and he returns to an enthusiasm for his old loves: the railways and snuffbox collecting which was the passion of his retirement.

It is only when one remembers just how long Vinsun has been retired that one realises his extraordinary longevity, for he left the railways in the early 1950s more than ten years before the steam trains began to disappear – and that was at the end of a career lasting just under half a century. But inevitably what fascinates Vinsun most these days are the changes he has seen in his lifetime.

'I can't remember the *first* motor car coming through our village,' he says, 'because I like to be precise about these things and I was busy playing somewhere, I think, when the shout went up that it was coming. I think I saw the back of it as it disappeared through the dust,

---

(Opposite) *A driver on the Great Central Railway in 1907; at this time drivers were regarded as a social élite, and this one is obviously proud of his responsible position, with his scrupulously clean oilcan and gold watch chain: punctuality was doubtless fastidiously maintained* (Hulton Deutsch)

BRITAIN'S OLDEST RAILWAYMAN

but I got a full view of the second car which seemed to be going at a hell of pace, though I shouldn't think it was more than five miles an hour. This would have been during the last decade of Victoria's reign.'

Vinsun's father was the village handyman – 'he did just about anything and everything' remembers Vinsun – and when he left school, Vinsun's decision to join the railway had more to do with simply taking the job that was available than with any love for steam. But that quickly changed as he began work on the great locomotives: 'I remember I cleaned the *Queen Alexandra* – the name of one of the engines – and it was a magnificent thing; most of our local engines didn't have names, they were just engines used for the local passenger and goods trains.'

It was to be some years before Vinsun graduated from cleaning and odd jobs to the footplate: 'When I started as a fireman I saw it as my chance to watch the driver and see how he did the job. At first of course it looked very complicated. You had to get the pressure just right to get the train to move at all. You had to learn to fire the engine properly, and of course certain types of coal were much better for this. On the LNER, which is where I moved later on in my career, I think it would be fair to say that our methods of locomotive practice were not as consistent as, say, those of the Great Western, but then they had better coal which could make a great difference. Theirs was relatively smokeless, which was good.

'One of the biggest changes I remember very early on was that Cunard, the shipping line, moved from Liverpool to Southampton and went from using coal to using oil. That reduced the price of coal considerably, but of course, although that was good for people who bought coal, it knocked Liverpool for six; in fact I don't think the city ever recovered.

'I passed fit for driving on Shrove Tuesday – I can't remember which year, but I remember it was Shrove Tuesday, and well before 1930. I'd certainly already been working for many years. The most exciting thing about it all, of course, was that it meant I earned a bit more money. I drove the trains from Gorton, and I drove them all over the place, to Glossop, Stalybridge, Macclesfield, Liverpool, all local stuff. Many of the lines I worked disappeared with the Beeching cuts. In those days, of course, we weren't romantic about steam; it was hard work, much harder than diesel or electric, and they were made – the engines, I mean – simply to do a job.'

During the Great War, Vinsun registered as a conscientious objector, which was an immensely unpopular thing to do at the time. 'I was examined several times before Judge Mellor who seemed fairly sympathetic. I simply stated my case and hoped for the best. And this was at a time when many conscientious objectors were imprisoned.'

Once he'd become a driver Vinsun found the work enjoyable, but he emphasises that in those days it was still only a job. The romance of the thing only came much later: 'Yes, I did enjoy it, because you had status; it was important work and looked exciting to others with different jobs – which is why so many children always wanted to be train drivers. Of course it really was exciting, too, despite the fact that it also had a lot of routine about it. And that's how I saw it. In recent years it's gone from being exciting to positively glamorous, which tickles me a bit!

'It's certainly fair to say that I was a rather good driver. No accidents and always very reliable – which is more than you can say for the brakes on those early trains! They often caused us problems compared with modern train brakes.

The handwritten text on the photograph reads: *The final steam engine at Altrincham Station*.

The last steam train at Altrincham station before the line was electrified in 1931
(Trafford Metropolitan Borough Council)

'After I retired I collected snuffboxes, which were still being used when I began my hobby! I collected dozens, and some were valuable. My daughter has them now.

'The thing I remember most about the steam trains was working at night, and how busy it could be then with goods trains moving everywhere. And in the wars – that is, the Great War and the Second World War – there was a shortage of uniforms so we always had to wear an official hat; as long as you had your hat, it didn't matter too much that you didn't have the rest of your uniform. Trains were very reliable then – apart from those brakes of course!

Having explained all this, Vinsun decides to sing me an old railway song; and then, as sprightly as an eighty-year-old, he looks at his watch, realises it's dinner time, and disappears under his own steam into the dining room.

NOTE Vinsun Gulliver died in August 1997.

Railways and Health

Very contrary opinions are held upon the effects of railway travelling upon the health of passengers. Dr. Walter Lewis, the medical officer of the London Post Office, in his Report issued in 1863, states that he has arrived at these conclusions from observations of the health of the travelling officers of the Post Office: that railway travel has little, if any, injurious effect on healthy, strong, well-built persons, if the amount be not excessive, and if they take moderate care of themselves; but that persons who take to habitual railway travelling after the age of 25 or 30 are more easily affected than those who begin earlier, and that the more advanced in age a traveller is, the more easily is he affected by this sort of locomotion. Weak, tall loosely-knit persons, and those suffering under various affections, more especially of the head, heart, and lungs, are very unsuited for habitual railway travelling.

Anon Good Things for Railway Readers, 1863

Loos and Luggage

As there were no WCs, travelling with children could be a trying experience. Families would secure a compartment to themselves and carry a chamber pot, as some mothers still do for young children. At the opening of the Newcastle and Carlisle Railway there were brass bands on the roofs of two of the carriages of the processional train. The practice of carrying luggage on the roofs had not ceased in my childhood (the late 1870s), and the rails to which it was roped or strapped, survived for some years. On our local Maryport & Carlisle Railway, Mr. Carrick, who had been looking into the matter, reports speeds as: express goods 40 miles an hour, passenger expresses 30, 'locals' 25, ordinary goods 20, and, on a branch 15.

J. W. Robertson Scott *The Day Before Yesterday*, the autobiography of the founding editor of *The Countryman* magazine, 1951

Trains on the Road

We have almost forgotten the fact now-a-days, but railways in their early years had to compete for passenger traffic with something besides stage coaches. 'Railroads, except in very peculiar circumstances, are behind the age,' says, in 1831, the author of a pamphlet written to prove the absurdity of building one between Edinburgh and Glasgow. He adds that the future is not on the side of cumbrous locomotives with their long, lumbering trains, but of

steam road-carriages – 'of which a great many are already required by coach proprietors, carriers of merchandise and others for their use on the public roads.'

Mr Scott Russell – afterwards the builder of the Great Eastern – established in 1834 'a line of steam coaches between Glasgow and Paisley as the regular mode of conveyance. These ran for many months with the greatest regularity and success and the trip, a distance of seven and a half miles was run in forty-five minutes.'

These steam coaches escaped the payment of tolls which were by act of parliament authorised to be levied upon all vehicles 'drawn by one or more horses or mules etc.' They were consequently the object of the fiercest hostility of the road trustees.

W. M. Acworth *Scottish Railways*, 1890

Highland Breakdowns

A breakdown on a railway is always a serious thing, but much more so when the line is single. So the Highland appliances for dealing with the interruptions of traffic are of the most elaborate nature. At Inverness there is kept a steam breakdown crane which can lift a weight of fifteen tons and move itself while at work. The machine must have cost thousands of pounds, but as the use for it may obviate the necessity of throwing three or four damaged carriages over an embankment in order to clear the line, the money may prove to be well spent.

W. M. Acworth *Scottish Railways*, 1890

Train Delays

'On Wednesday last, a respectably dressed young man was seen to go to the Shoreditch terminus Eastern Counties Railway and deliberately take a ticket for Cambridge. He has not since been heard of. No motive has been assigned for his rash act.'

Such was the language in which *Punch*, a generation back, gave utterance to the popular sentiment about the line that nowadays, having changed both its nature and its name, is known as the Great Eastern; nor is there any reason to suppose the satire to have been one whit more trenchant than was in fact deserved. Certainly, it stood by no means alone. 'The scapegoat of companies, the pariah of railways, the Eastern Counties' is the phrase employed without any justification being thought necessary by Francis in his *History of the English Railway* which was published in 1851. It was of the Eastern Counties that the tale was originally told, how a ticket collector,

11. The opening of the Liverpool and Manchester Railway, 1830.

expostulating that a strapping lad of sixteen could surely not be entitled to travel half price, was met by the rejoinder that he was under twelve when the train started! Even a journey on the Eastern Counties, said the novelist Thackeray, must have an end at last.

George P. Neele *Railway Reminiscences*, 1904

Grease for Goods Wagons

The ingredients consist of palm oil, soap, soda, tallow and small quantities of the finest castor oil. They are turned by the barrowload into a huge boiler. This boiler is jacketed with steam and the inner liner is perforated so that jets of live steam can be admitted all round. More water is added to bring the mixture to the required consistency – thicker or thinner according to the weather and the time of year – and then the whole is made to boil freely after which it is drawn off into shallow vats and left for a day or two to cool and harden. Finally it is dug out and placed in casks. For the use of its forty-five thousand wagons the Caledonian railway manufactures some six to seven hundred tons of grease per annum.

W. M. Acworth *Scottish Railways*, 1890

What's in a Name?

It is worth while setting down, because almost forgotten since the amalgamations which preceded the coming into existence of British Railways, the now unfamiliar names of some of the railways by which I travelled at one time or another in my childhood, youth and young manhood.

They included the Maryport and Carlisle, the North British, the Caledonian, the Highland, the North Eastern (which took over the Carlisle to Newcastle-on-Tyne), the London & North Western, the Midland, the Great Northern, the Great Western and the Great Eastern, which amalgamated with the North Eastern. From London to the south-east coast there was silly strife between the South Eastern and the London, Chatham & Dover, nicknamed because of its accidents, the London, Smash-'em & Turn 'em-over.

When I came into the world in 1870 there were a hundred and thirty different railways!

J. W. Robertson Scott *The Day Before Yesterday*, the autobiography of the founding editor of *The Countryman* magazine, 1951

Railways and Cholera

On Monday last the Hawick branch of the North British Railway was opened throughout for passenger traffic. The opening was attended with no public demonstration, the ravages of the cholera having been so severe.

The Scotsman, 31 October 1849

Ticket Error

My first experience of railway work commenced in the booking office at Ely Station and my first attempt at issuing tickets without supervision was made in the absence of the upper clerk who was training me. He was late coming on duty and in order to advance matters I booked the passengers who were waiting for the train. Unfortunately, I issued penny-per-mile tickets instead of the third class which in those days were, on some lines, obtainable by trains not appointed to call at every station. My instructor came in at the last moment and, discovering the mistake, at once rushed out to the platform and obtained, fortunately for me, the difference in cash from the passengers and exchanged the erroneous tickets for correct ones.

George P. Neele *Railway Reminiscences*, 1904

Positions on the Coal Sheet

It should be explained that all the drivers doing the same class of work, working for instance the broad gauge expresses between London and Swindon are formed into one corps technically known as a link. Every pound of coal and every pint of oil that goes into each man's engine is debited to him, and at the end of the week the total is made up and divided by the number of miles his engine has run. The men are then arranged in order of merit, that is, of economy of fuel and oil consumption, on a sheet hung up on the notice board of the running shed.

Of course for a single week, extra load or stress of wind, greasy rails or what not, may affect a man's position, but in the long run (assuming every man's engine to be in equally good condition) the man who comes out top is the best driver, in other words, is the man who can do his work to time – for punctuality, of course, comes before coal saving – with the most scientific economy of force. In fact, a driver feels the loss of a good position on the coal sheet much as a boy feels on being sent to the bottom of his form at school.

George P. Neele *Railway Reminiscences*, 1904

Out of the Ark

It was only yesterday, but what a gulf between now and then. Then was the old world. Stage coaches, more or less swift riding-horses, pack-horses, high-waymen, Druids, Ancient Britons. All these belong to the old period. I will concede a halt in the midst of it and allow that gunpowder and printing tended to modernise the world. But your railroad starts a new era. We who lived before railways and survive out of the ancient world, are like Father Noah and his family out of the ark.

William Makepeace Thackeray, 1860

Gurney's Steam Carriage.

The Great Railway Hotel

The passenger who is kept waiting at Perth Station Hotel must admit that there is not much fault to be found with the accommodation there provided for him. Even the very dogs are not forgotten and after their hot night in the train, should enjoy their roomy kennels with fresh water and clean straw. For their masters there are comfortable dressing rooms with baths all complete, while downstairs the breakfast, with its never ending relays of fresh Tay salmon, can fairly challenge comparison with the famous bouill-abaisse of the Marseilles buffet.

W. M. Acworth *Scottish Railways*, 1890

Class Struggle

The early first-class carriages were made to repre- sent three coach bodies joined together. At the end, outside, was a seat for the guard. Every railway had second-class compartments. The earliest second-class carriage, like the third-class carriages, had no sides, the roof being supported by iron pillars. The passengers therefore suffered from wind and rain.

Mr. Gladstone, in retiring from the Presidency of the Board of Trade, said 'the Board had not proposed any alteration in the form of third-class carriages, but had insisted that they should be provided with seats, and should be covered in from the weather', with the characteristically Gladstonian proviso 'as far as was consistent with the necessary admission of light and air'.

For some time, on expresses, there were no third-class (or 'Parliamentary') carriages. Early thirds in the provinces (and on the London Underground) were without partitions, and, at the time I went to London, it was possible for boys, in the absence of many passengers, to clamber over the wooden seats from one end of a carriage to the other. The seats were pencilled, often rudely, and also hacked by mis- chievous adults as well as idle lads. Later on, in the third-class carriages, rather thin cushions appeared on the hard seats. The cushions got cut and torn; electric-light bulbs would certainly have been smashed. These third-class compartments had no window straps. For first-class and second-class pas- sengers, in an age much given to hawking and spit- ting, there were spittoons. Thirds spat on the floor. Third-class passengers' trains had sometimes to wait for hours while the gentlemen's trains went by.

J. W. Robertson Scott *The Day Before Yesterday*, the autobiography of the founding editor of *The Countryman* magazine, 1951

Unconstitutional

'I consider,' said Mr Weller, 'that the rail is uncon- stitootional and an inwasion o' priwileges...'

Charles Dickens *Master Humphrey's Clock*, 1840

Carriage Lighting

The oil lamps, enclosed in heavy glass containers, about nine inches in diameter, hung through holes in the carriage roofs, and were dropped into their places by a man who got to the roof of the car- riages by steps at the end. The glass lamps, wheeled along the platform in a bogey truck, which had frames for them to rest in, were thrown up to the man on the carriage roofs, who caught them with a bit of cotton waste in one hand in order to prevent their slipping. After him came a man who walked along the roofs to light the lamps.

Children were naturally much interested in all this. I recall how the iron lids over the holes through which the glass containers hung were crashed down. These lids, which had catches to prevent them from rattling, were not level with the carriage roofs, but were at the top of little cylinders like iron top hats. When the train was in motion the oil sometimes leaked and sloshed about in the lamp containers, and the light from what Thomas Hardy called 'the roof lamp's oily flame', was often dim. This was either because it was not burning well or because of the scratching and rubbing the glass got when the lamps were changed in the absence of the special truck and were set down on the platform. Sometimes a lamp would go out or be for some time at the point of giv- ing out.

It was usual, when starting on a journey, to walk the length of the platform in order to find a seat in a compartment with the best prospect of illumination. But when gas was introduced as an illuminant in Queen Victoria's train it is stated that Her Majesty required that oil lighting should be restored. She thought it safer.

J. W. Robertson Scott *The Day Before Yesterday*, the autobiography of the founding editor of *The Countryman* magazine, 1951

Early Engines

Early railway engines differed in appearance from modern locomotives in that their bodies were lower and their smoke stacks were narrow, and as tall as would go through the tunnels. The driving wheels were also as high as possible, quite eight feet.

The railway engine of the period may be seen in Turner's painting 'Rain, Steam and Speed' or in Frith's 'Railway Station'.

> J. W. Robertson Scott *The Day Before Yesterday*, the autobiography of the founding editor of *The Countryman* magazine, 1951

Railway Matrimony

Among other great advantages afforded by railways has been that of opening out the great matrimonial market, whereby people can pick and choose wives all over the world, instead of having to pursue the old system of always marrying a neighbour's child. So we now have an amalgamation of countries and counties, and a consequent improvement in society – improvement in wit, improvement in wine, improvement in 'wittles', improvement in everything.

> R. S. Surtees *Mr Facey Romford's Hounds*, 1864

Cutting through Camden

The first shock of a great earthquake had, just at that period, rent the whole neighbourhood to its centre. Traces of its course were visible on every side. Houses were knocked down; streets broken through and stopped; deep pits and trenches dug in the ground; enormous heaps of earth and clay thrown up; buildings that were undermined and shaking, propped by great beams of wood. Here, a chaos of carts, overthrown and jumbled together, lay topsy-turvy at the bottom of a steep unnatural hill; there confused treasures of iron soaked and rusted in something that had accidentally become a pond. Everywhere were bridges that led nowhere; thoroughfares that were wholly impassable; Babel towers of chimneys, wanting half their height; temporary wooden houses and enclosures, in the most unlikely situations; carcasses of ragged tenements, and fragments of unfinished walls and arches, and piles of scaffolding, and wildernesses of bricks, and giant forms of cranes, and tripods straddling above nothing. There were a hundred thousand shapes and substances of incompleteness, wildly mingled out of their places, upside down, burrowing in the earth, aspiring in the air, mouldering in the water, and unintelligible as any dream. Hot springs and fiery eruptions, the usual attendants upon earthquakes, lent their contributions to the scene. Boiling water hissed and heaved within dilapidated walls, whence, also, the glare and roar of flames came issuing forth; and mounds of ashes blocked up rights of way, and wholly changed the law and custom of the neighbourhood.

In short, the as yet unfinished and unopened railroad was in progress; and, from the very core of all this dire disorder, trailed smoothly away upon its mighty course of civilization and improvement.

> Charles Dickens *Dombey and Son*, 1846

Steam Trials

Steam engines for drawing wagons were attempted here, but unfortunately at the trial of the second one, it burst and killed thirteen and wounded an immense number more, one of whom was Mr Steele, and some of the owners.

> From an unpublished manuscript dated 1815, on the Durham mines

Mushrooms in the Tunnel

There is another less necessary article of food than meat, which the North British Railways deals with in wholesale quantities, and that is mushrooms. It comes about in this wise. The old Edinburgh, Perth and Dundee line got into Waverley by a tunnel under St Andrews Square and Princes Street.

It was about three quarters of a mile long and the gradient so steep as to necessitate the employment of a stationary engine. Of late years a detour out to the east has avoided the gradient and the tunnel has been abandoned. Two years back an ingenious person conceived the idea of leasing the tunnel and growing mushrooms – the railway company were not too exacting about terms as they knew they would be paid to carry the materials for the hotbeds in and the mushrooms out. When I was there one bitter cold day last March, I found a huge fire of anthracite burning just inside the lower mouth of the tunnel. In

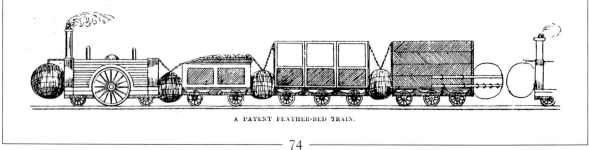

A PATENT FEATHER-BED TRAIN.

IN THE SIDINGS

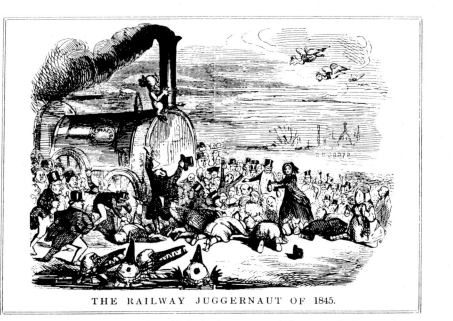

THE RAILWAY JUGGERNAUT OF 1845.

In a Punch *cartoon, the citizens of England surrender their savings to the Juggernaut of railway speculation.*

this way the chill was taken off the air as it entered the tunnel. What used to be the up line is kept clear for mushroom beds. I learned that at the time of my visit in March the French growers had not yet got their produce into the market and that the Edinburgh Mushroom company could obtain 1 shilling to 1 shilling and ninepence a pound and even at that price had more orders than they were able to execute.

W. M. Acworth *Scottish Railways*, 1890

Heating Carriages

In cold weather iron foot-warmers were supposed to be supplied. They were about two-and-a-half feet long by three-quarters of a foot wide, and four inches deep, and were filled with what had been boiling water. They had handles at both ends, by which they could be lifted into the compartments by the porters. As there were seldom enough of the foot warmers for all the compartments in a train, it was usual to tip the man who looked after them. On a long journey the foot-warmers, which when hot were not supposed to be good for one's boots – for we wore boots then – seldom kept warm long enough. They might indeed become too cold for one's feet to rest on them, and passengers made efforts at the stations stopped at to get them changed. The doors of some compartments fitted so badly that snow drifted below them or wet came in. In bitter weather one

could be very cold indeed. At stopping places, passengers' expostulations about bad light or about cold (or leaky) foot-warmers involved a good deal of disagreeable window-opening. In winter, a traveller wore a heavy ulster and had with him a rug, and sometimes put on a tweed cap, called a fore-and-aft or deerstalker, the flaps of which let down over his ears, as may be seen in the cartoons of the period.

J. W. Robertson Scott *The Day Before Yesterday*, the autobiography of the founding editor of *The Countryman* magazine, 1951

Granite Plateway

To my mind, the greatest curiosity of all railway works is the granite plate-way which was built from the Haytor stone quarries on Dartmoor to Newton Abbot. This was strictly speaking a *plate-way* and not a railway although it was built as late as 1821 (which was after the invention of the latter). The difference is that in the plate-way (which was devised about the middle of the eighteenth century) you don't employ flanged wheels. If it is made of iron, an L-shaped section was used. The trucks had flat tyres like road vehicles. The units of the runway were called plates and not rails, a name which we still preserve in 'plate-layer'.

Edmund Vale *Curiosities of Town and Countryside*, 1940

Fish-Bellied Rail

The fish-bellied rail is of course rare, though a track still laid with it is to be seen alongside the main line of the LNER north of Darlington. Kirby Muxloe station (LMS) in Leicestershire has the front of its platforms built up with square stones that are perforated. These are the original sleepers of the Leicester and Swannington Railway which was surveyed by George Stephenson. The engineer was then engaged in the construction of the Liverpool and Manchester Railway and refused to undertake this one as well, so his son Robert, who was only twenty-seven, got the job – the first of his many great works. The sleepers are just square blocks of stone that were placed diamond-wise at short intervals between the 'bellies' under each rail, the gauge being maintained by the ballast. They started off with only one locomotive – the *Comet*, which was built in George Stephenson's works at Newcastle and sent by sea and canal to Leicester. Passengers had not been thought of – only coal. But presently they provided one passenger coach and issued a set of tickets made of brass which were collected by the guard and returned to the stations which issued them on the return journey. It was owing to a collision between the *Comet* and a farmer's trap on this railway that the first locomotive whistle came into existence. After the mishap, Mr Ashlen Bagster, who managed the line, asked George Stephenson if he could not fit the engine with some sort of trumpet to be blown by steam. Stephenson regarded this as something within the province of a musician and not an engineer, so a musical instrument maker in King Street, Leicester, was entrusted with the design of the steam trumpet. No doubt he tried to pitch it as melodiously as the old mail-guard's post horn, but the pressure of the steam made him fall back on the cruder principle of a whistle.

Edmund Vale *Curiosities of Town and Countryside*, 1940

Guards on the Roof

The guards of branch trains had a rougher time of it than those of the present day. The brakes of the trains were worked from the roof of the carriages, the guards riding outside, in an unprotected seat at the end of the vehicle, applying the brake by turning on the hand screw. A journey from Wymondham to Dereham cured me of my desire to travel outside railway carriages.

At the end of the train were two of the vehicles with outside seats for the guard. They were so marshalled that the seats became vis-a-vis. The guard, an old stager, sat on the one which enabled him to turn his back to the engine, while I, as a novice, sat opposite, facing him. The dust, the smoke, steam, and smother, which filled my eyes, ears, and nose during that short ride, were sufficient to put a stop to any wish for further experience in that direction.

The accommodation for guards has certainly vastly improved since those days. After a while the roof seat had a small box-shaped shelter for the men, and I have seen a small rough curtain added, so as to shelter them still further from the weather. The open van was the next advance, a vehicle having one end covered and suited for the reception of luggage and parcels, the other end open and fitted with a small seat for the guard, having the brake wheel close at hand. These vans were accustomed to be turned on the tables with which all terminal stations were provided, and thus the guards travelled at the end of the train, ceasing to be exposed to the necessity of facing the engine.

The double-ended vans did away with the necessity for turning vehicles, and have led to the provision of thoroughly well sheltered vehicles, with padded seats, lighted compartments, and apparatus for warming food while travelling – a striking contrast to the old style. I was surprised, when in America (in 1881), to find the system of working the brake on to vehicles from the roof still in force, not, indeed, with the passenger trains, but with the goods trains, the large covered freight cars having brake-screw handles on their roofs, the 'Brakeman' passing along the top of the vehicles, applying the brakes when necessary, a very dangerous business in rough weather, and especially so on lines where tunnels exist; but as a protective warning, overhanging gantries with pendant whipcord pellets, are provided not far from the tunnels, so that the men on the roofs, experiencing the warning stroke of these pellets, may lie down while passing through.

George P. Neele *Railway Reminiscences*, 1904

Coal Savings

Sometimes a bonus is given to the fireman who does his work efficiently upon a supply less than usual. One great railway company has issued a circular pointing out to their firemen what an enormous economy would be effected if each of them saved one pound of coal per mile.

But taking into consideration the many kinds of work a locomotive fireman is called upon to do, the fact that coal only costs an average of ten pence per mile is rather creditable. Water, one half penny, and oil, one farthing, per mile, are other average costs.

S. T. James *The Railwayman*, 1928

THE BRAKE
VAN MAN

JOHN KERLEY

Guard on the London &
North Eastern Railway

In the old days, according to John Kerley, the driver drove the train but the guard was in charge of it. Immensely proud of his forty-odd years on the railways, John, now seventy-three, is saddened by the fact that the guard no longer plays such a vital role; but he's also grateful that he knew the railway industry when the train was still king of the transport system. He was born in the street where he still lives, and his first job on leaving school at the age of fourteen was as an electrician's mate. He was immediately thrown into one of the busiest periods of his life, as most of London's houses were in the process of being converted from gas lighting to electricity, a process that continued throughout the 1930s.

Tiring of the electrician's life, John worked in a dairy, making pats of butter. Then war started and he joined the Navy. It wasn't until he was twenty-five that he finally found the career that suited him – and this is perhaps rather surprising, given that several members of his family were already employed on the railways: his wife's uncle, her father and his aunt, to name just a few: 'My father-in-law was a loco inspector, and he was sure I'd enjoy working on the railways. He was pretty convincing, too. They were also crying out for staff at the time so it wasn't too difficult to get a job. I was interviewed at King's Cross and my first job was awful – I had to do shifts that started at 1am or 2am or 3am: that was all they gave me because the night trains had to be covered, and the last man to be taken on always started at the bottom in every respect.'

John spent the first three weeks of his career as a porter at Hatfield. He sorted parcels, swept the platforms and helped people with their luggage: 'I did all the basic things. Despite what most people think, carrying people's luggage was not really part of the porter's work; we called it weaselling because you were really trying to ingratiate yourself to get a tip.'

After just three weeks at Hatfield, John left portering behind and was sent to King's Cross as a trainee guard. He spent four weeks working with an experienced guard to get used to the various duties and routines: 'I'd start at 8am by reporting to the guard superintendent who'd tell me which guard to report to. Then I'd be shown the sidings, because guards guarded the train as well as the passengers. We were responsible for backing trains into sidings – they were never driven in, always backed in, with the guard directing operations and signalling to the driver who, of course, couldn't really see where he was going. It could be tricky, too, reversing into the sidings, because you had to know all the signals and setbacks.

'There were no phones either, in those days, which meant that you had to use hand signals and lamps to get the driver to do what you wanted him to do. After four weeks I was put in front of the signals inspector who quizzed me on all the rules and regulations and working practices. I found it all a bit of an ordeal; inspectors in those days always seemed solemn and very important, but I think I passed all right simply because I'd had a really good teacher. The guards in those days really knew their stuff. The other curious thing about this time was that you decided yourself when you were ready to go in front of the inspector. Might sound a funny way to do it, but it actually worked very well because it put the onus on *you* to learn fast.'

From King's Cross, John went to Barnet and Enfield where he spent much of his time shunting in the sidings. These were the days before roads and container lorries had begun to eat into the railways' almost total domination of transport. Thus at Barnet and Enfield there were sidings everywhere, and so many coaches that they were kept off the road for as much as six months at a time.

'In these early days,' remembers John, 'I worked mostly on what was called the empty coach link, the shift of men who brought empty coaches into London or took them out from London to Barnet and Enfield and the sidings. When we put the coaches together we had to check all the electrical connections to make sure all the lighting and so on would work, as well as the vacuum and steam pipes. We'd also check that windows were closed and handbrakes off. As guards working in the shunting yards we were so busy we hardly had time to breathe; it was mucky work, too, but we were never given overalls, and this always struck me as odd – firemen, cleaners and drivers all got overalls, but not us. Just one of the peculiarities of the old railway, I suppose.'

But John is keen to emphasise that drivers relied heavily on the skill and experience of the guard. And if the mainline guard knew which guard had checked the train and put it together, he'd know whether or not to make his own checks. These days, on the other hand, as John himself points out, the guard is a sort of glorified ticket collector:

'In my day the guard was an important man, vital to the safe operation of the train. There

The King's Cross guards' rest room in 1951, with John on the far left

were three links among the guards: the lowest, where we all started, was the empty coach link when you were simply getting coaches ready and bringing them to where they needed to be. Then, strictly according to seniority, you moved up to the local link, which meant you worked on trains doing local runs; and finally the top link meant you were on mainline trains. There were also two volunteer links, for the Newcastle and Edinburgh run – they were volunteer because you had to lodge away from home, but they paid extra.

'Trains were machine-washed every day if they were going to the sidings at Hornsey; but if they were destined for Holloway they weren't washed by machine, they were all washed by hand, simply because there were enough people to do the work!'

Like drivers, guards had to know the road before they were allowed out. John learned the road to various places from King's Cross – places like Peterborough – and then had to sign a legally binding document to confirm it. Placing the responsibility on the individual in this way was important as lives depended on it, in a very real sense. John and his fellow guards used to make their own 'road books', notebooks in which they drew the various routes and lines, and the positions of signals and crossings on them.

'There were always moments of drama, too – I remember trains occasionally lost steam on a steep incline north of Wood Green in North London where what we called a jack catch was installed. This was a device designed to derail a train that lost all steam and began to slip back. We used N2 steam engines for local work, and on another incline, this time towards Finsbury Park, they'd get stuck occasionally if they hadn't had a run at the hill or if the sand was poor and the line wet.

'If the train stopped here we used to leap out and put detonators on the track, the idea being that when a relief train approached to give us a hand, it would know how close it was to the stalled engine as it backed into position. The rescue engine driver would then blow what we called a cock crow on his whistle before he got going with the stalled train behind him. I'd usually be out there with a lamp helping when this sort of thing happened – and I remember, too, it was awful if you had to do all this in a tunnel, because the noise of the detonators used to bring down great falls of soot from the tunnel roof; by the time you got out you were covered in the stuff. The drivers hated the noise of the detonators going off in tunnels, too, and they'd try to get you to put down fewer than you were supposed to.'

As time went by John found that he could spot problems long before they arose, although that didn't always mean he was able to do anything about them. For instance, 'At Wood Green I could always tell when a train was about to get stuck – we'd have a run at the hill, and if the engine and first carriage got over the top of the hill I knew we were all right; but if only the engine got over, we were in trouble.' In a situation like this the train stopping would mean delay and serious disruption to the timetable. Drivers, guards and firemen always hated unpunctuality – but despite the best efforts of all concerned, things still, occasionally, went wrong. It was the price that had to be paid for a railway system that relied heavily on the skills of train crews and on what by today's standards were remarkably primitive, if magnificent, engines.

'Drivers, and everyone else for that matter, were very proud of their good time-keeping, which is probably why we didn't get stuck that often. When it did happen, I'd walk back to the nearest signalbox so the signalman knew we'd blocked the line up ahead. The guard always had a vacuum brake in his van and that went down, too, if the train was stuck. When you think that the old Pullman train might weigh 440 tons you can see that they took some pulling, and that there were bound to be problems now and then; certainly the sand would always be running as we approached a hill. Certain things were not such a problem in the steam days as they are now: wet leaves, for example, because the old engines would crush through the leaves. Diesels are lighter and don't crush through so they are more likely to slip. Snow was always more of a problem with diesel electrics, too, because it used to make their motors short out, something that obviously could never happen with steam trains. The only problem with snow in the steam era was that it mucked up the mechanical signalling.

'I remember on the 7.45am to Leeds once there was so much snow that we didn't get back till three o'clock the following morning. That was caused by two feet of snow, and with that much, all the signals broke down and you had to crawl along. You had to stop at *every* light and go back and protect your train with detonators under what was called time interval service; and of course as a result of all this, journeys would be badly delayed.'

With electronic signalling unaffected by weather, the responsibilities of all railway workers, but especially guards and porters, have been greatly reduced – and that, of course, means that the jobs are more mundane, and so less satisfying than they were.

John also points out that guards and drivers were often quite close in their relationship because they relied on each other: 'They trusted each other because they had to. I remember some marvellous drivers. There was Tiddler Wilson, for example, a wonderful man, who was so short he had the regulator bent in order to reach it. The other reason you tended to work closely with the drivers was that you worked regularly with the same small group of men, and a lot of people knew each other or were even related to each other. On the local link, I worked mostly with ten drivers, and my wife's uncle was one of them.'

When the present Duke of Kent got married, John was the guard on the VIP train that took Winston Churchill and Clement Atlee to York where the wedding took place; it was packed with dignitaries and MPs, most of whom John remembers as friendly and courteous. At one time or another he has also met Lord Home, Harold Wilson, Ted Heath and numerous football teams!

'In those days almost everyone went by train,' he says wistfully. 'Prince Philip was a frequent rail traveller, and he always seemed to be in a hurry when I saw him, striding along and oblivious to everything. Famous people could be surprisingly forthcoming, too; I remember being astonished early one Sunday morning to find Douglas Home – he was then foreign secretary, so it must have been late 1950s or early 1960s – waiting for his car. We started chatting, and he told me what he was planning to do as foreign minister. I suppose he was really just thinking aloud, but I was terrified for a minute that he might ask my advice!'

Despite the early years of unsocial shift work and low pay, John stuck at the job and began

June 1961: John was proud to take his place as one of the guards on the Royal Train on the occasion of the Duke and Duchess of Kent's wedding

to move slowly up the links. He also began to enjoy himself, although the level of responsibility never diminished: 'Bowling along in the guard's van was enjoyable once you were on a good link, but I had six big journals to keep up to date – all the stations we passed and the times at which we passed them had to be filled in, and even in the dark you always had to know where you were. Twenty minutes were allowed for the King's Cross to Hatfield journey, and if we were late I was held to account for it; a couple of yellow signals followed by a red would all be logged in one of my books as evidence for delays. I might even attribute delay to the driver if I felt he wasn't driving particularly well. The book, or journal, was seen by every area you passed through so that all information could, if necessary, be corroborated.'

British Railways had standardised brake vans by the mid-1950s, and they were fitted with a periscope so the guard could see over the top. Earlier guards' vans had a sort of bulge at the top fitted with windows; but despite greater visibility and improved equipment, mishaps still occurred, though they were rare; for instance: 'I can remember approaching Arlsey in Hertfordshire when part of the motionwork came off the train – a side rod had come away from the engine. One end was still attached and the other was smashing into the gravel ballast at the side of the rail and throwing huge amounts of it up and over the carriages; I could hear it raining down on the roof. That was a nasty incident, because if the rod had come off completely the train would probably have been derailed. Luckily it stayed on long enough for us to be able to stop.'

One interesting little trick remembered by John was the use of scent bottles to give advance warning of bearings overheating, often the cause of serious failure. These small bottles of scent were fitted next to the motions under the boiler – if the motionwork got too hot, the bottle broke, and the driver smelled the evaporating scent and knew he had a problem. John was always fascinated by the ancient heating systems on the old steam trains, but he is adamant that, in most cases, they did their job. In fact these trains were heated directly by steam from the engine itself:

'On a very cold winter's day,' explains John, 'you had to watch it because if you lost power you lost heat, too, for the passengers. The steam went through thick pipes under the seats. I knew when we were in trouble because at the back of the train I needed 20lb pressure at

'...a side rod had come away
from the engine.'

least, and if it got below that I knew it was time to start worrying. In my time I worked on N1s, N2s, J50s and J52s, A1s, A2s, A3s and A4s – just about everything. The best was the A3, I think; the drivers loved them too, because they provided a good ride.

'Guards' vans were always freezing, though; until British standard vans came in you had a little cubby hole in the corner of the van with a tiny heater and a little coal fire that would get white hot sometimes, with the draught created by our speed. In the guard's van in the early days you also had a little cooker where you cooked your breakfast. I'd always managed a very nice fry-up by the time we got to Peterborough!'

By 1957 John was working in the top guards' link at King's Cross, with the mainline passenger trains: 'It's a curious thing, and I'm by no means saying it was a good thing, but in those days everyone – train drivers, guards, porters and engineers – went to the pub at lunchtime and had a beer or two, and there were never, or very rarely, any accidents. But then railways were not just a way to make a living, they were a way of life. That's why when it snowed you would often find guards, supervisors, porters and other station staff helping out. I think we had a lot of pride in the job because we always seemed to be doing things we didn't really have to do.

'The funniest thing I can remember was being told to get a bunch of yobos out of a first-class compartment; so I went along, but having checked their tickets discovered it was Jimi Hendrix and his entourage!' But what looked like trouble sometimes really did turn out to be trouble – like the time John came across a particularly rowdy individual on the train to Peterborough. With no telephone or other means to get help he used his wits – and a potato!

'I couldn't think what else to do, so I wrapped a message round a spud and threw it to the next signalman, who telegraphed ahead. The trouble-maker was booted off when we got to Peterborough.'

From his very earliest days John remembers men who would have started work in the early part of the century, such as Old Gore the stationmaster at King's Cross who always wore a top hat and tails, and always saw the *Flying Scotsman* off in person at 10am on Fridays. In many ways the railway year was divided up by the seasons and special dates for which special trains had to be provided; thus there would be excursion trains in summer, and at King's Cross, special trains for the opening of the grouse shooting season: 'August 12 seemed to cause a mass evacuation to the moors of the north by wealthy Londoners,' says John with a grin. 'The trains were packed with sportsmen. They'd turn up with half a ton of stuff – dogs, guns, hampers and countless bags.'

Like many railwaymen, John welcomed the new diesel engines when they began to appear, but he soon realised that in the very process of solving old problems, they created new ones: 'They robbed us of overtime, for a start, because they were quicker – too quick, if you ask me! And they had no magic about them, just simple efficiency. Even at the time people realised that.'

As the steam trains disappeared and were replaced by diesel, so other changes took place at King's Cross, not least the vast increase in the numbers of railway enthusiasts: 'Train-spotters always struck me as a bit of an oddity,' says John, 'because they knew far more about the engines than any railwayman ever did; some of those kids were there every day of the

(Previous page) King's Cross station in 1953, with the Doncaster train about to leave

NIGHT TRAINS TO SCOTLAND FOR THE TWELFTH

The finest fleet of trains in the world steams North to Scotland every day and is specially augmented for the 12th. Day and night they leave Euston, King's Cross and St. Pancras with their restaurants and sleeping-cars (first and third class) and their excellent staffs of servants. Below is a full list of night trains. Times of day trains will be supplied on request at any L M S or L·N·E·R station or office.

FROM EUSTON (L M S)

WEEKDAYS

P.M.
7.20 AB "The Royal Highlander"—Perth, Boat of Garten, Inverness, Aberdeen.
7.30 AB Oban.
7.40 AB Stirling, Gleneagles, Dundee.
8.0 A Dumfries, Stranraer Harbour, Turnberry.
9.25 Glasgow (On Saturdays, Third Class Sleeping Accommodation only).
10.50 Edinburgh, Stirling, Gleneagles, Perth, Dundee, Aberdeen, Inverness.
11.45 "Night Scot"—Glasgow.

A.M.
12.30 DE Dumfries, Kilmarnock, Glasgow.

SUNDAYS

P.M.
7.20 B "The Royal Highlander"—Perth, Boat of Garten, Inverness.
7.30 B Stirling, Oban, Gleneagles, Perth, Dundee, Aberdeen.
8.30 Dumfries, Stranraer Turnberry.
9.30 Glasgow (Cent.).
10.50 Edinburgh, Stirling, Gleneagles, Perth, Dundee, Aberdeen, Oban.
11.45 "Night Scot"—Glasgow.

NOTES : A Saturdays excepted. B Dining Car Euston to Crewe. D Saturday nights and Sunday mornings excepted. E Sleeping Cars to Kilmarnock.

FROM KING'S CROSS (L·N·E·R)

WEEKDAYS AND SUNDAYS

P.M.
*7.25 R "The Highlandman"—Edinburgh, Fort William (Breakfast car attached en route) Perth, Inverness.
*7.40 R "The Aberdonian"—Edinburgh, Dundee, Aberdeen, Elgin, Lossiemouth.
†10.25 "The Night Scotsman"—Glasgow. Dundee, Aberdeen, Perth.

P.M.
†10.35 Edinburgh, Glasgow. (North Berwick. First class only and on Friday nights only.)

A.M.
§1.5 After-Theatre Sleeping and Breakfast Car Train. Edinburgh, Glasgow, Dundee, Aberdeen, Perth, Inverness.

Nightly (except Saturdays). † Nightly. § Daily (except Sunday mornings). R Restaurant Car King's Cross to York.

FROM ST. PANCRAS (L M S)

WEEKDAYS

P.M.
9.15 Edinburgh, Perth, Aberdeen, Inverness.
.30 Dumfries, Kilmarnock and Glasgow (St. Enoch).

SUNDAYS

P.M.
9.15 Edinburgh, Perth, Aberdeen, Inverness.
9.30 Dumfries, Kilmarnock and Glasgow (St. Enoch).

With a return ticket to Scotland, you now have the choice of travelling back by the East Coast, West Coast, or Midland routes, with break of journey at any station. PENNY A MILE SUMMER TICKETS are issued every day (first class only two thirds higher) for return any time within one month—break your journey at any station. Ask at any L·N·E·R or L M S Station or Office for Pocket Timetables and Programme of Circular Tours

IT'S QUICKER BY RAIL

LONDON MIDLAND & SCOTTISH RAILWAY
LONDON & NORTH EASTERN RAILWAY

week, and they not only knew every engine, but they knew exactly where it had come from!'

John was eventually promoted to cleaning supervisor, which put him in charge, but took him off the trains themselves. Though the job was less interesting, it did, however, bring him into contact with some unusual passengers – such as twenty Miss World entrants – 'I didn't think much of them, actually,' says John.

By the 1970s John had been promoted to operating assistant at Bounds Green, his last job before retirement in 1989. He'd completed forty years, and never really wanted to retire: 'Being a guard meant you got well known, particularly among the drivers. It was a serious job, but we had a lot of fun and I can tell you that guards were probably the best domino players in the world!'

John has also achieved a certain immortality through a derailment on the north-east line at a place called Offord: as he was on the train that was derailed, the spot became known as 'Kerley's Corner'. But John's most solemn memory is of the arrival at King's Cross of the funeral train of King George VI. All the pillars in the station had been draped with purple and the station was absolutely silent. 'All you could hear were the quiet commands of the officer in charge,' says John, 'and then the slow march of the pallbearers.'

The old railway was full of anomalies and quirky working practices that by modern standards seem almost bizarre; even John was baffled occasionally. 'I could never understand why guards were issued with a watch, while drivers were not. I've always supposed – but it's a bit of a guess – that it was because once the driver knew the road he would drive almost by instinct, whereas us poor guards had to fill in precise times in our ledgers.'

MEMORIES OF GREASE CORNER

BILL SIDWELL

Engineer on the London Midland & Scottish Railway

Bill Sidwell lives happily in retirement at Caversham in Berkshire. He started work on the railway in 1927 aged sixteen. Born in 1911 in Lincoln, he moved with his parents to Derby, then at the heart of the railway industry in Britain, when he was two. His immediate family had no connection with the railways (although an uncle had been a signalman) but transport, in the form of early motor lorries, provided employment for his father. 'Dad was one of the last people, in fact, to drive a lorry with solid rubber tyres and no windscreen. Lorries were an unusual sight at that time, as most road transport was still by horse-drawn wagon. My dad had started work as a chauffeur at about the turn of the century when cars were also a novelty on the road.'

Living in Derby, then one of the biggest railway centres in Britain, it was almost a foregone conclusion that Bill should go into railway work; he'd always been interested in the practical side of things, so when he left school, he chose to start as an apprentice engineer at the Derby locomotive works. Day one saw him in the machine shop, in grease corner, as it was known: 'I was set to work putting threads

The erecting shop at Derby locomotive works in 1938
(National Railway Museum)

on nuts – that's what everyone started on in those days. Everything seemed to be done in vast quantities of oil; at the end of the first week I was absolutely covered in the stuff.' Bill laughs loudly at the memory, and this reaction is typical of his tolerant and amused view of life.

After that grubby introduction he moved around through the various departments and workshops: machine shop, boiler shop, erecting shop, foundry. This was where the practical work was done, the work that kept the railway functioning. His next move was to what was then known as the progress office: 'This is where the work was all planned, and it's from here that the instructions and orders for work emanated. What struck me most about it was how meticulous and thorough everything seemed to be.'

After a few months he saw a sign on a noticeboard inviting people to apply for what was called a 'privileged apprenticeship'. Having only recently left grammar school he thought he might have a chance. He applied, was accepted, and to this day chuckles at what the job involved. 'Well, it was ridiculous really, because all the privilege part of it meant was that you spent two and a half days each week at technical college and got absolutely no pay for it!'

During the 1920s and 1930s there was no set pattern of progress toward the goal of fully qualified fitter or engineer; it all depended on vacancies and seniority. It was only much later that a proper training course was instituted. But for now, Bill was happy in his new role: 'Our chief engineer was Sir Henry Fowler, and I remember he got all us privileged apprentices together one day and said he'd agreed a big concession for us: instead of disappearing for two and a half days each week – unpaid, if you recall! – we would now be sent off to technical college one day a week. And the really good news was that we still wouldn't be paid for it!'

In Derby the atmosphere of the trains was everywhere – 'they absolutely dominated the town,' says Bill – and once you'd started work in the industry it would have been highly unusual to have opted out and tried something else, as Bill explains: 'Well, a lot of it had to do with the Depression in the 1930s. You were so lucky to have a job of any sort that you counted your lucky stars and never even thought about changing. Apart from anything else, in Derby there wasn't much else to do anyway. When I started, the other problem was that the country was still on the road to recovery from the Great War, and when you did get a job there was no career structure or career planning involved as there is today; no one thought about such things.

'My father first spoke to a local builder about getting me a job. At that time most boys left school at fourteen, but I'd won a scholarship to the local grammar school so I got another two years. The builder I might have gone to work for had a relative who worked on the railway, and he suggested I apply for the apprenticeship. I remember being asked at the interview what I eventually wanted. I said I wanted to be a draughtsman, but the man interviewing me put "fitter" on the paper. I don't think he liked the idea of my getting a bit above myself!'

Bill was apprenticed for five years, and he knew that to improve his chances of future promotion he would need to get a technical qualification: 'You had to pass at a number of things,' he recalls. 'For example, technical drawing was a major part of the apprenticeship – I remember it took up about half our time, as well as three evenings a week. At the end of the five years I got what I suppose would be the equivalent of a BSc today. It was a pretty thorough course: we dealt with the mechanics of fluids, higher maths, the structure of metals – the whole lot. I got my college diploma and then joined the Institute of Mechanical Engineers, and ultimately I qualified as a fellow of the institute; that was a proud moment.'

A 4F 0–6–0 locomotive under construction at Derby locomotive works in 1926 (National Railway Museum)

Bill's engineering skills, although certainly comparable to those needed for general construction, were actually directed at fulfilling the needs of the industry that dominated the town in which he'd been brought up. It's difficult to imagine, now that so much heavy industry has closed down, that Derby was almost entirely taken up with the railway in the early part of this century, and that by the 1930s some six thousand people worked in the carriage works, and another six thousand in the railways proper. But despite the demand for qualified people, jobs were still scarce. 'A lot of apprentices were simply discharged at the end of their five years,' explains Bill. 'You had no guarantee of a job at the end. Some of those who weren't required went to Rolls Royce who were just starting up in Derby. I remember we all used to go into town on the trams which ran in from all directions. We lived in a village called Challaston a few miles outside Derby, and I saw the tram lines laid to my village and I lived to see them all dug up again. Challaston was on a branch line which closed in 1929, so for my first two years I went by train, thereafter on the tram. I was pleased about the tram coming really, because the train station was quite a way from my home – a lot of villagestations tended to be quite a distance from the centre of the village. There were buses, too, and I think it was the buses that really killed the local railway.

The 'Crabs' were the first mixed traffic Moguls for the LMS, and could be seen all over the Derby area from the late 1920s; the example seen here is hauling a passenger train at Ambergate, north of Derby (Milepost)

The works canteen in the late 1940s (Derby Museums & Art Gallery Industrial Museum)

'I was one of the lucky ones, and when I'd finished my training I was asked if I wanted to go in what was called the Motive Power Department. I was accepted here and went to London immediately for eighteen months.'

In London, Bill continued his training. He was based in Camden, to the north of the City, and the next year and a half was spent doing three-month stints in different departments: three months with the fitters, whose job it was to examine and repair the locomotives; three months with the shed staff cleaning boilers; three months with the running foreman, the man who told the drivers where they were going; and finally three months on the footplate on shunters, local passenger trains and passenger expresses out of Euston.

'I remember there was no difference in status between drivers of expresses and drivers of local trains,' he recalls. 'If an express driver pulled up alongside a shunting engine at Euston and the driver shouted over to the shunting engine driver, "What price your little loco?" the little loco driver would always shout back, "Same as yours – ninety bob a week!" I enjoyed those eighteen months enormously; I met some wonderful old Cockney characters and had some marvellous experiences on the footplate. The pay was rotten, of course – in fact it was barely enough to pay for my digs in Chalk Farm. If I remember rightly my digs were about thirty bob a week and my pay sixty-five bob.

'Footplate work was undoubtedly the most interesting aspect of the work, but it was uncomfortable. I don't think people realise how uncomfortable it was, and they certainly don't if they never travelled on it themselves; you were more or less open to the elements, it was noisy and dirty, and it could also be very bumpy. But I remember how impressed I was when I saw the way a loco picked up water in a scoop while moving – although it didn't always go as smoothly as it did the first time I saw it; one day for instance I was on the footplate heading towards London when the locomotive failed and we had to change it at Derby. We got going again on a London North Western Prince of Wales, only to find that we were soon short of steam. We put the water scoop down and then found we couldn't get it up again, with the result that we got half a ton of water over *us* – the whole footplate was absolutely soaked!

'On another occasion we were going to what was then known as London Road Manchester (it's now Manchester Piccadilly) on a Royal Scott-type loco called *Girl Guide* – I remember it was No 6169 – and we'd just stopped at the buffers at London Road Manchester. We were watching the passengers leave the station when a little old lady noticed the name of the loco and smiled up at us. "How nice," she said, "I used to be a girl guide." I remember the old driver mumbled after she'd left, "God help any girl guide whose as rough as this old girl!" What he meant was that the Royal Scott was a good engine but it was bloody uncomfortable to ride in. A lot of London Midland engines were very rough riding. Great Western engines were definitely better; they had a few shortcomings but no Great Western man would ever admit it or tell you what they were!'

After his eighteen months in London, Bill set off back to Derby to the old headquarters of the LMS for a period in what was called the shopping bureau. This was where the engines were repaired and where essential maintenance work was carried out, including major overhauls. The thing that struck Bill most was the skill of the men in the workshops: 'I spent a few months here, and then went back to Euston doing the same work, more or less. Seeing how those men kept the engines going was a lesson; they knew them inside out and would make light work of what, to a newcomer, looked impossibly difficult.'

Next stop for Bill was Rugby: 'They moved everyone a lot in those days, from the highest to the lowest. It would have been about 1935 when I got back to my home town, and there I came across a man in the works who was doing what was called a work study. Basically he was a sort of time-and-motion man, looking at how we did things, and assessing whether they could be done more efficiently. I was made part of the study and I had to time the fitters at their various tasks – and that didn't go down well, I can tell you! I did nine months of that. It was interesting, though nothing compared to being on the footplate.'

Eventually Bill was put in charge of a depot at Widnes, Lancashire, as a running shed foreman, a job that was later re-christened shedmaster. Nine months later he did the same job at Llandudno Junction, where he was made assistant supervisor: 'I remember one Christmas Eve I'd got permission to go home on the two o'clock train once the afternoon foreman had relieved me. He turned up at two o'clock prompt and I went off to catch my train – only to discover that there was no locomotive to be found. This was particularly funny as I was supposed to be in charge of making sure that all the engines were where they should be at the appropriate time. I rang the controller, and more by luck than judgement, managed to get a freight train that was at Rhyll. We brought it down, turned it round and I was at home for Christmas – but only just!

'Just before I left Llandudno Junction a chap rang from Crewe to tell me I'd been given a post elsewhere. For some reason which escapes me now he couldn't tell me exactly where, but he explained that I would receive the details in a letter. The letter duly arrived and off

I went to Mirfield in Yorkshire. I was to be shift foreman: my first proper staff appointment. All the others had been in the way of gaining experience and training. There were three shifts here, from midnight to 8am, 8am to 4pm, and 4pm to midnight, but luckily the running shed foreman did the midnight to 8am shift. I worked six days a week, but not Sundays.'

Bill found that he'd been thrown in at the deep end: he spent every minute rushing around making sure all the locomotives were being properly serviced, and making sure the right drivers and firemen turned up at the right time, and all this had to be done to time. Mirfield had local passenger work to Leeds, Huddersfield and Holmfirth, and of course there were specials and excursion trains to organise:

'I was there in 1937, the coronation year of George VI. The coronation was on the Thursday before Whit Sunday and it was a national holiday so we ran specials to Blackpool. On Whit Sunday morning I got a call to say we'd been asked to supply fifty specials for Blackpool on the Monday. "How many can you do?" I was asked. I finished by being able to offer about thirteen, but we had to use six double-home drivers – that is, drivers who lodged away from home. Also, from Mirfield there are twenty-seven variations of the route to Blackpool, if you can believe it, so I had to make sure that each driver knew the particular route he was going to take. It was a bit of a nightmare, but we got there in the end!'

This was the sort of pressure on which Bill thrived, but in addition to problems caused by timetabling and organisation, there was the sheer graft of engineering work that had to go on twenty-four hours a day if the trains were to be able to do their job:

'From an engineering point of view a steam engine presents interesting problems,' says Bill. 'From cold, it takes eight hours to get an engine ready to go. The reason is, that you've got two to three thousand gallons of water to be heated before anything can happen, and that water has to reach boiling point under pressure before you can move anything. We had men called steam raisers to get the locomotives going from cold. The steam raiser was told what time the engine was needed, and it was then left to him to start work at a time that would ensure the train would go out on time. He'd start the fire by putting a bit of wood and a few rags in – it really was as simple a starting point as that, just like starting a coal fire at home. With a steam engine, of course, he'd keep adding coal until he had a hell of a blaze going and the water had reached the required temperature.

'Once the water was boiling you could put on the blower to improve the draught; that made more heat, but burnt more coal. One trick on the midnight shift when you were firing engines for 6am was to put your hand on the ash pan – if that was warm you knew all would be well for the morning. At Mirfield we had sixty locomotives and one steam raiser per shift, but a good man could do a lot on his own.'

On the London Midland steam raisers were not employed, and the firemen were expected to fire the engines themselves. This was also known as fire-dropping. It was a very dirty job, and it is one of the reasons why Bill, like so many steam railwaymen, considers that the men welcomed diesel when it came in. Whatever the pleasures of driving steam trains there is no doubt that one or two jobs, like fire-dropping and boiler washing, really didn't have anything to recommend them; indeed by the 1950s it had become increasingly difficult to get people to do this sort of work at all. In the 1930s when jobs were in short supply it didn't matter how dirty the job was – you could always get someone to do it.

'Boiler washing was a filthy job,' says Bill, 'but loco boilers were still always cleaned once a week or once a fortnight. On the Western Region we didn't go in for water softening which some areas had. Where you used soft water it meant a loco boiler only had to be washed perhaps once a month. This was a big saving because it can take twelve hours to wash a boiler properly.'

After Mirfield, Bill was given a shed at Oldham in Lancashire: 'More moving round the country,' he says with a grin. 'It never seemed to stop, and they'd almost expect you to go anywhere. At Oldham I looked after twenty-three locomotives. It's difficult to say exactly how many loco sheds there were nationally at this time, but there would have been eighty or ninety districts, each with five or six sheds, so that gives you some idea. Most towns had their own locomotive depot.'

From Oldham, Bill went to Manchester as a locomotive inspector; he was there from 1938 until 1944. During the war the railways really came into their own because there was no petrol for private cars: 'Everyone relied on us, which is why, like many railwaymen, I couldn't be released for war service because ours was a reserved occupation. Mind you, judging by the way railways were targeted by the Germans I don't think we got off that lightly; the Manchester office got blitzed and an awful lot of depots were damaged in the war. Many were never rebuilt.

'When we knew war was inevitable I was given the job of supplying every depot with what we called anti-glare sheets. These were blackout sheets, made out of canvas that had been treated with waterproofing; each one had to have fittings for the various classes of engine, and I had to make sure it all went smoothly. On the railways, as pretty much in every walk of life, the war created a great feeling of camaraderie.'

Towards the end of the war Bill went as an assistant district locomotive superintendent to Gloucester; the job involved freight traffic to the ports, and he was there from 1944 to 1949 looking after seventy engines as well as several sub-depots. 'I was at Gloucester in 1948 when nationalisation came and I can honestly say it made absolutely no difference to me; but on the dot of midnight on the day it happened, all the trains in the area blew their whistles. I remember my phone ringing at around this time, about a train that had been derailed on the Great Western. We were the London and Midland, but we had a crane that would be suitable for this particular derailment. When the person on the other end of the line asked for the crane he said he wanted it for the British Railways Board, and this sounded so strange because it was the first time I'd heard the name.'

Bill thinks nationalisation was a good thing in many ways; for instance, it helped speed up the exchange of information and ideas between different areas. Financially, however, it made little initial difference. 'When nationalisation took effect the railways were very run down, largely because of the war and the lack of funds that resulted from it. Before that the government had always taken the profits the railways had made, but they never put anything back; to some extent that situation continued when nationalisation came, too, and the move from steam to diesel was all done on a shoestring. Some railways even toyed with the idea of running buses – they had quite a fleet for taking stuff from various depots. To my mind, rail never went sufficiently in search of business because for so long, and particularly during the war, they'd had a virtual monopoly on transport.'

Nationalisation also meant that, at last, standard locomotives began to be built, and they were still being built as diesel trains began to come in. After various jobs in different parts of the country Bill ended up back in London; and then in 1963, a decision was taken to cease classifying footplate staff as engineers. Instead they were placed under the control of

3440 City of Truro *at Old Oak Common in 1957; this locomotive achieved a speed of 102mph on the descent of Wellington Bank, Somerset, in May 1905*

operations, a recognition, it seems, of the difference between being a steam-train driver and a diesel or electric driver.

'People were excited about the new diesel trains because of the novelty, but they created as many problems as they solved. Apart from anything else, there were so many different kinds of diesel engine, and there was no attempt to be consistent when it came to buying them. The last of our steam engines – I'd inherited some five hundred at Old Oak Common in West London in 1959 – ran from Oxford to Birmingham. In many respects I was sad at the end.'

The most memorable event in Bill's forty-five years' service came on the day that Winston Churchill was buried in 1965. 'That was an extraordinary day in every respect: so much meticulous planning went into it, but we only narrowly avoided a very embarrassing incident. I had the responsibility of making sure the funeral train stopped at precisely the right spot so that the bearer party could get the coffin out and down the ramp. The train stopped just right as it turned out, but when the guardsmen in the train tried to open the doors from the inside, their combined weight – they were all standing on the side of the train by the doors – tipped the coach over so far that the door wouldn't open. Nothing happened for a few seconds, then the Duke of Norfolk marched up and asked what was going on. I'd hidden six platelayers nearby in case there was trouble, so they rushed up and moved the wooden ramp which had been jamming the doors. Once the doors were open, the ramp went back and the ceremony could continue. With the television cameras there and people watching all over the world, it was a tense moment, I can tell you!

'Another incident I remember well involved the royal train. It used to come through regularly, but on this particular occasion the present Queen and Prince Philip were on a three-day visit to the Worcester area. They were sleeping on the train and we had to stable it on a branch line just the other side of Worcester itself; it was about midnight, and we were at the branch line waiting for the train to arrive. It came into view, and then at that *very* minute we heard three shots. Immediately all hell broke loose – the train stopped and everyone seemed to panic. The three shots were to signify danger: we knew they weren't gunshots, they were detonators, but that might mean another train was on a collision course.

'Anyway we discovered that a platelayer had put the shots down because a horse had jumped on the line. So we got a tow-rope and set off after the horse which, luckily, we found quite quickly. But heaven knows what the royal party must have thought when they heard those bangs!

'Each region had its own royal train in those days, but I think Prince Charles is the member of the royal family who still uses the one remaining royal train.

'The other royal train I remember particularly was the *King George VI* which carried the

1952: the funeral train of George VI leaving Paddington station

body of the king from Paddington in 1952. I remember the men lining up along the track-side and all along the platform with their caps off. Mind you, that train wasn't the *King George VI* at all – the real *King George VI* was being repaired at the time, so we took the name-plate off it and put it on another train. I don't think that's ever been revealed before. We nearly had a problem, too, because that engine had to be kept ready to go for a long time, with plenty of steam and so on – but it was also important that it didn't make too much noise; and as the delay lengthened, we thought we might have to let her get rid of some steam, and that would have made a terrible racket. Anyway, we got the band to play again (and loudly!) and we put more water in, and that just about did the trick until we were ready to go.'

Bill has nothing but praise for the men he worked with over the years – 'the drivers were a great bunch, to a man,' he insists – and whether a problem arose with a royal train or a humble freight wagon, someone could always be found to sort the situation out. But as in all walks of life, the railway organisation was subject to human error: 'Most accidents that I can recall – and there were regular freight derailments – were due to human error. The worst I remember happened on Sharnbrook Viaduct near Bedford, when the signalman let a one-hundred-wagon coal train through and it ran into another coal train. The loco and tender and thirty wagons swept over the side of the viaduct, and the driver and fireman were killed; it was a terrible mess. However, when you think that the whole system in the steam days was run using only men and mechanical aids, it is a tribute to their skill that so few accidents actually did occur.'

Fortunately accidents, like this one at Oakley Viaduct in 1949, were rare

FROM FIREMAN TO FOREMAN

RAY BEESON

Driver on the Southern Railway

Ray Beeson, now a decidedly youthful-looking sixty-three, started his working life as an engine cleaner at Guildford station in Surrey in 1950. 'It was just a job,' he says with a smile, 'and there was certainly no family interest in the railways; but once you'd joined you knew you were part of something a bit special.'

Ray's father was a policeman who didn't want his son to follow him into the force: 'I suppose that, apart from being steered away from the police, it was just luck or fate that took me to trains,' he says now. He grew up at Chilworth, in Surrey, and trains ran past the end of the family garden so the sound of the railway may well have worked its way into his subconscious; this idea he finds faintly amusing, but can't quite bring himself to reject outright.

'I left school in 1950 and the railway seemed a good, secure job. I started as a cleaner because that was the first rung of the ladder, but it was an important job. In those days trains had to be spotless before they went out, and nationally, I should think thousands of us were employed in this way since it was a job done almost completely by hand; we did it all with paraffin and oily cloths, and no part of an engine was left untouched. When you first started you had to clean up under what we called the motions – the wheels, pistons and so on – and it was absolutely filthy work; but if the driver came along and saw that some part of the engine wasn't clean he'd make you go back and do it again. No driver wanted to take out a dirty engine. You had to do the outside as well, of course. The length of time it took to clean each engine would obviously depend on the sort you were dealing with – the biggest at Guildford in those days was the U-class, and the smallest was the M7 tank engine. We had C3s, too – we called them Charlies, and they went from one to forty. Qs were really just wartime engines, and weren't meant to be used once we'd stopped fighting the Germans; but they were actually kept in regular service for another twenty years after the war ended. They were very powerful because they'd been made to pull tank trains. On average we reckoned to clean two locos in an eight-hour shift; that would be a team of half a dozen of us, so you can see, it was a thorough business.'

For a man who joined the railways with no real enthusiasm for trains, Ray has developed something of a passion for them, and there's nothing he enjoys more than a long chat about the ins and outs of steam working. He also has a great memory for odd details – like the resident tube cleaner at Guildford who jealously guarded his own special iron rod with a brush on the end. Though it is now long gone, the Guildford shed once housed something like thirty locomotives, used both for freight and passenger work. Ray quickly realised that here, as elsewhere, seniority was the only route to promotion, although he was quite happy to bide his time.

'It took me ten years to progress to being a fireman, but that was pretty standard in those days. You started by getting just a few turns as a fireman, and then when you'd done enough turns, they made you a passed cleaner, which in my case meant I was working roughly

50 per cent of the time as a fireman and 50 per cent as a cleaner.

'The fire was always lit by the time the firemen arrived, but it wasn't the sort of fire that you could use to get the train going; it was really just a little bundle of flame right inside the door that just kept the thing warm and gave you a start. I always used to begin by opening the door and simply spreading around what little fire there was; that was the first step on the way to building up your steam. It used to take about an hour to get up sufficient steam to move the engine, but during this time there were lots of other things to do: it was a routine of checks and procedures. You'd get oil for the driver, and you'd check the smokebox, making sure it was nice and tight – if it was loose you'd hear a sort of suction noise and it would be difficult to make steam. You'd watch the pressure gauge until it reached somewhere between 120lb and 220lb per square inch, though on engines for the big Channel packets you might have to get up 240lb or more. If I remember right, it was 180lb on the U-class and about 220lb on the Q-class. Q-class engines were used for goods work where, typically, you might be working with sixty-five wagons behind you. Keeping an eye on your steam was vital because you were on a booked time – if your steam wasn't sufficient to get you going at the right time, then all the other trains behind you could be disrupted.

'Firemen signed on at the same time as their drivers, and we always did eight-hour shifts, with a start at 2am, or 4am, or the early shift which was one minute past midnight.'

Passed cleaners were frequently expected to change back and forth from cleaning to firing from day to day, but once they'd reached a stage where they were no longer doing any

An M7 tank engine at Guildford station; the driver lived in one of the houses on the skyline

cleaning – in other words, by the time they were fully-fledged firemen – they were treated with more consistency, particularly when it came to shift working, as Ray explains: 'A fireman could expect to start at the same time each day for at least a week, unless he had to cover a rest day or something.'

Ray believes there are many misconceptions about the role of the fireman, particularly the idea that the job meant hours of unrelenting shovelling on the footplate. He argues that in fact there was nearly always time to stop and think when you were firing: 'If you knew what you were doing, I suppose you could describe the job as keeping the fire topped up, once you were underway, and how frequently you had to top up would depend on the weight of the load and the quality of the coal. There *were* times, though they weren't too frequent, when you *were* pretty nearly shovelling for all you were worth – the Waterloo to Basingstoke, Bournemouth and Salisbury run with ten coaches is a good example; on that run you were pushed to get the odd minute between bouts of firing.'

The fireman at Guildford, as elsewhere, had a wide range of duties, but they were all concentrated on enabling the driver to do his work; it was very much a team effort, as Ray explains: 'I don't know what people did in other areas, but teamwork was definitely the key

word on my patch. When it was foggy, for example, and you couldn't see the semaphore signals, you'd both of you, driver and fireman, be desperately keeping a lookout. It was all right on the mainline, or at least it was better, because they had coloured lights, but on the less important lines – say, Woking to Basingstoke – it was all semaphore which was a nightmare when visibility was poor.'

For Ray, one of the great pleasures of the footplate was simply the sense of speed, the warmth on hot days, and the exhilaration of firing on crisp, frosty mornings: 'On a bright winter morning it was wonderful when you had time to look about a bit as you steamed along – though of course that was only true when you were going engine first; if you were the other way round – that is, tender first – you'd be so cold that I can assure you there was no pleasure in it at all!'

In summer the footplate could be unbearably hot until the train had picked up sufficient speed to pull a breeze through; but winter or summer, Ray was always astonished, particularly in his early firing days, by how well the drivers knew every inch of the road: 'They always knew exactly where to start braking on every gradient.' Mind you, the process of bringing the train to a halt was also a big part of the fireman's job; with loose-coupled

A typical 1950s scene with a Brighton to Cardiff express, which would have passed through Ray's domain in Salisbury en route (Milepost);
(inset) a Q1 locomotive and wagon at Cranleigh station, which no longer exists

freight wagons, which had no brakes of their own, Ray would start braking using the turned handbrake on the tender. 'That would bring the wagons together, so you'd have captured the whole weight of the train ready for the driver to put the engine brake on.'

Ray's own memory of the area he worked is still detailed and thorough despite the fact that he has now been retired for a number of years; but of course it is the difficult parts that he recollects most clearly: 'One or two bits of our area were notorious – Virginia Water Bank between Reading and Feltham was really extremely difficult, and there was a very steep section between Reading and Redhill known as Dorking Bank. It was places like those two that made it absolutely essential that you knew the road and your engine; if you didn't, you would almost certainly get stuck on that Reading to Redhill section, with all the timetable consequences that that would entail for your passengers and all the passengers in the trains behind you.

'There were different skills, too, with passenger as opposed to freight working: with freight you had to start braking a lot earlier because of all those loose-coupled wagons with no brakes, whereas passenger trains all had continuous brakes on all carriages. The guard at the back of the train would know all the gradients, too, and his brake van would come into operation.'

The area Ray covered was Guildford to Salisbury via Waterloo, but it also included Southampton, Redhill and Bournemouth; it was the heart of the Southern Region. After a number of years firing – he can't remember quite how many – Ray became a passed fireman, to all intents and purposes a driver. A few years later he took over as relief foreman at Guildford locomotive shed. 'That meant that one day I would be working as foreman

The Brighton terriers were one of the best loved types on the Southern Railway (Milepost)

Ray in the early 1960s

and the next I'd be back driving.' As it turned out, Ray was the last foreman at Guildford loco shed before it closed for good.

'People at Guildford didn't like change, and it was particularly unsettling when Guildford closed as a depot and we all went to Woking. Southern Region was unusual in that we'd had some electric trains since as early as the 1930s; they were clean and efficient, but they didn't have the character of steam. I drove some of these early electric trains – you just had to push a button and that was it. With steam it was more unpredictable even though we knew what we were doing; it relied more on intuition and judgement, and of course things did go wrong occasionally, however good you were. Sometimes you just ran out of steam, and you'd then have to stop, build up your steam again and then off you'd go.'

Ray is annoyed by the commonly held belief that steam locomotives were completely lacking in fail-safe systems, and he goes to great pains to explain how at least one of these systems worked: 'If your steam pressure got too low the brakes came on automatically, and if your water got too low a lead plug would be melted by the heat of the fire and whatever water was left would crash down on your fire, put it out and the whole thing would shut down, thus avoiding an explosion. This was very rare though – it never happened to me, and I was never involved in a crash, either.'

During his time as a driver Ray worked passenger and freight trains, and he recalls the working practices of the past as if this was all still a central part of his life. 'Well, it all became so much a part of your life that you knew it without thinking about it. We were in rostered links, twelve pairs of men in each link, and each week your link would do a different shift and work on a different line. The top link did all the best shifts, and you only got into the top link through seniority; thus the longer you were around, the better your chance of moving up – but it was very much a question of dead men's shoes because you only moved up when someone else died or retired. But at least it was the same for everyone, so there were few complaints. The only alternative was to try to get promotion by going to another depot. People didn't get made redundant in those days and some people were happy to stay where they were; others wanted to move and get on, and you certainly got the chances if you did that.

'Some men were desperate to work the electric trains, but not me! I was more than happy with steam. Kids were always coming up to the cab and asking for a ride, and we used to let them come with us – and unless you've travelled on the footplate as a child it's impossible to imagine the excitement of it. It was all more relaxed in those days – you wouldn't dream of giving a kid a ride in the cab today, you'd be sacked. We had some lovely runs, too – I

always enjoyed Redhill to Reading because it was such beautiful country.'

The latter part of Ray's career included stints as a relief train crew supervisor, and station supervisor at Woking where he was responsible for platform safety and for looking after the platform staff. He then became a train crew supervisor looking after crews, finding engines for them, organising special trains, and finding cover if a driver went sick. 'I enjoyed that because I was back working with the blokes who actually drove the trains. My last job was as relief stationmaster: I covered Woking, Surbiton, Basingstoke, Guildford and Haslemere whenever the regular stationmaster was ill or on holiday.'

Ray spent the last few years of his career helping with the rebuilding of Guildford Station, a job which he knew would make him surplus to requirements once it was completed. 'I'd taken on the job of assistant stationmaster, but the new station didn't need an assistant, so I suppose I built myself out of a job! I had a few other jobs before I finally retired; I was what was called a 'task force manager', supervising men who cleaned the stations in my area.'

Like many railwaymen, Ray has particularly strong memories of the fuss the imminent arrival of the royal train in the area would cause. Usually these trains were on their way to Southampton, with a specially appointed driver and top security all along the route, as Ray explains: 'There would be armed police on every bridge under which the train had to pass, and absolutely everything else moved out of the way long before the train got anywhere near us – nothing was booked to move in the area. We also always had a standby engine waiting along the route in case the royal train broke down. Sometimes a spare engine would follow the royal train all the way.

'But my happiest memories are of firing and driving steam engines; they gave you a real sense of achievement, and if you wanted to get home at night it was up to you and your skill. You couldn't just press a button. Mind you, when I was depot foreman I also enjoyed that. We used to wear a trilby and a blue smock – but that's now gone the way of steam, too!'

A COUNTRY STATIONMASTER

CLIFF CARR

Stationmaster on the London Midland
& Scottish Railway

Cliff (second left) *with his colleagues at Eardisley*

Like many bright young men in the 1940s, Cliff Carr won a place at the local grammar school, only to have to give it up to help support his family. Cliff was born in Llangattock near Crickhowell in 1926. His father was a miner who did not relish the prospect of his son going into the same industry. However, it was the death of Cliff's mother in 1940 that propelled him out of school and into the railways where he was to spend the rest of his working life. His first job, for which he was accepted only after passing a thorough exam, was as a junior clerk in Brynmawr where he stayed for two years, from 1942 until 1944.

'It was quite a journey to Brynmawr from my home: I had to cycle four miles to Gilwern and then push my bike half a mile up a steep hill before catching the 8.10 train which consisted of four vestibule-type coaches dating back to the early 1930s, and a Webb 0-6-2 coal tank engine. The ticket inspector here was terribly strict – he once reported me for not having a pass for my bicycle, even though he knew I was entitled to one!'

The line to Brynmawr climbs to over one thousand feet, and Cliff still remembers the glorious views in summer: 'They almost made up for the freezing temperatures in winter,' he says with a smile. The booking office at Brynmawr was unusual. Known as a Passimeter, it was wooden and glass, measured 12ft by 8ft and had a built-in foot-operated pedal that unlocked the gates controlling passengers' entry to the platforms. All booking had to be entered in a traffic book which was added up and checked daily, weekly and monthly. Cliff continues:

'Passenger trains were absolutely packed when they came through, especially on a Tuesday since this was market day in nearby Abergavenny. In fact when it was this busy the Webb 0-6-2 engines were replaced by LNWR 0-8-0 engines in order to haul an additional two coaches, making a six-coach train instead of the usual four.'

After six months at Brynmawr, Cliff moved on to Ebbw Vale where Dai Morris, the senior clerk, was such a suspicious character that his fingers had worn deep grooves in the underside of the wooden drawer where he kept his personal things. 'He was always tugging at it to make sure it was locked,' remembers Cliff.

In February 1944, Cliff was called up for war service; clerical grades, unlike signalmen and drivers, were not reserved occupations. He was sent to the Warwickshire Regiment for six weeks' intensive training. 'It was a bit of a shock,' he says now, 'but I didn't regret it in the long run. After six weeks they looked at my employment record, such as it was, and decided that, as a railwayman, I should be sent to the Royal Engineers, to what was called the Movement Control Section.'

'...the Webb 0–6–2 engines were replaced by LNWR 0–8–0 engines in order to haul an additional two coaches'

Eardisley station in 1920: Ernie Brooks (seated, right) *was a clerk there from 1918 to 1948, except for a three-year break when he worked in Brecon*

His first posting, in June 1944, was to the London Docks, and then he went to Willesden in North London where he helped supervise the loading of tanks and other military equipment onto trains. Then in September 1944, after the D-Day landings, he was sent to France: 'I was astonished while working on the European railways at how they used horse-boxes for the troops; each van had a sign saying "Sixteen Horses or Thirty Men", and they were truly relics of World War I!'

Next stop for Cliff was Belgium with the Second Army; here he worked at one of their main depots from which ammunition trains were sent to Holland for the troops in the front line. 'My railway experience did actually prove useful because I knew how to keep good records and was able to liaise with the Belgian Railway people – I was even able to use my grammar school French. The Army weren't daft when they made these decisions.'

By May 1945 he was on the Rhine organising movements of coal. Then suddenly he was sent back to Britain for a few weeks before being ordered to the Far East via Tobruk and Bombay: 'I ended up in Java, in what was then still known as the Dutch East Indies, help-ing to organise tank and troop movements because the Japanese war was still on. I reckon 90 per cent of the people I worked with were railwaymen, and I wonder to this day if the role of the railwayman at home and overseas in wartime has ever really been given the attention it deserves in books about the war. After all, nothing could move without us, and the more efficiently we did our job the better for the war effort.'

By the end of 1947 Cliff had completed his four years, and he was sent back to England

and discharged. 'I had two months' leave and then reported back to Swansea Victoria, the headquarters of the LMS in South Wales. I think they were a bit surprised when I just turned up and asked what post they had for me. They knew that, under wartime regulations, they had to keep a job open for me, so they sent me to Eardisley on the Hereford and Brecon Line. I was made a class five clerk, which might sound very grand until you remember the complexity of the railway hierarchy and that a class five clerk was the bottom grade!'

Eardisley was a small country station, and Cliff arrived in November 1947, knowing no one in the area. He remembers a foggy, freezing day and a long walk into the village, for the station was well outside Eardisley itself. But if the place seemed remote and the weather unpropitious, the staff were very different:

'You would have to go a long way to meet a man as pleasant as dear Ernie Brooks who was to be my stationmaster. He was about sixty when I first met him at Eardisley. He was a real old-style railwayman, friendly and helpful and really one of the most endearing chaps I've ever worked with. It shows you how different things were in the old days, because when I arrived at Eardisley in my early twenties I was on the same grade as Ernie had been until very recently, and he'd worked for the railway for decades. They were hard times, and promotion was hard to get.'

Ernie had just been promoted to stationmaster and Cliff took over his old job. The two men were the only clerical staff at Eardisley, but there were also signalmen and porters and goods staff. Ernie and Cliff were also responsible for keeping an eye on Kinnersley Station and Whitney-on-Wye, both local stations.

'I had to deal with passenger, goods and parcel traffic,' says Cliff, 'and I remember thinking at the time that clerical work at small country stations gave you a real insight into how railways really worked; it was as if you could see the structure on which everything else was based. We used to book tickets for passengers and organise the work in the goods office, dealing mostly with farm produce – grain, hay, sugar beet and so on. There were animal food stores from which local agents sold to farmers. The food arrived in bulk and was delivered by railway lorry, or the agents used their own transport. Some farmers collected their own feedstuffs.'

The system of which Cliff was now an integral part had been built up over decades and it was designed to ensure that nothing went astray: 'It's difficult to visualise now,' says Cliff, 'but road transport accounted for a much smaller percentage of the movement of goods in those early days. A huge amount of small stuff, even supplies for the local greengrocer, would come in by train, together with farm implements, animals, milk,

Leading porter Bill Eccleston at Kinnersley station in 1959; Kinnersley and Credenhill battled fiercely for top prize in the best-kept station competition

fruit and every other kind of local produce you can think of. The most perishable produce, for obvious reasons, came on the passenger trains, not on the goods trains.'

Together with his stationmaster, Cliff was responsible for paying twenty men in the area; these included platelayers, maintenance men, station repairers, signalmen and shunters. They also paid themselves. 'We certainly did, but like everything else it was all checked by the district office.' As a class five clerk Cliff was paid less than a porter. He received just £5 a week, and it took six years to reach the maximum pay for the grade which was £8. Half his wage went to pay for his lodgings so things were difficult, but as he began to take part in the social life of the village, things took a turn for the better: 'I hated Eardisley at first, but came to love it. I met my wife there, went dancing regularly in the village hall and even played football for Hay-on-Wye and cricket for Hereford.'

Cliff quickly realised that to get promoted he would have to move, and he admits he was ambitious. He began studying the rules and regulations for signalling and for railway accountancy. He was given a promotion, but found that the district office in the Eardisley region wouldn't release him for the post as they were unable to replace him. Under the railway agreements that existed at the time, if he couldn't be moved to his promotional post, he had to be put onto the top salary for his existing job. Then in October 1951 he moved to Hay-on-Wye as chief clerk. He stayed here until 1954 – 'my new stationmaster boss was far stricter and less friendly than Mr Brooks!' – and then decided that he should try to become a stationmaster himself:

'That was much more difficult than it sounds because I was only about twenty-six and the era of younger stationmasters was only just beginning. I knew I would have to accept a post for which there was less competition. Vacancies were advertised weekly on a list and I started applying for every post with a stationmaster's house – and this was important as I'd married in 1952 and we had a baby son.'

But Cliff was determined, and in 1954 he was appointed to his first job as stationmaster. The station was Nantybwch, and he recalls: 'I hated it there. Nothing to do with the work, but I'd grown to love the Herefordshire countryside and I found my new environment difficult to get used to. My wife didn't like it much either.'

At Nantybwch it was all passenger traffic, and Cliff had to look after his own station and Rhymney Bridge; both had signalboxes controlling single line junctions with double lines. One of Cliff's biggest responsibilities was to make sure the colliers' trains ran punctually. There were two on each shift (early afternoons and night), and it was vital that these trains were not delayed as the Coal Board imposed fines for lateness. 'Once or twice I was glad that I knew enough about signalling to get us out of a difficulty,' remembers Cliff. 'When the signalman didn't turn up on one occasion I was able to open the box and get the colliers' train going on time.'

Nantybwch was famous for its dreadful winter weather, so much so that the permanent-way staff were sometimes on snow and frost duty for weeks on end, and on one never-to-be forgotten day a pile of huge stones fell from a bridge a few miles from the station and almost derailed a train. For six weeks after that buses were used while the bridge was demolished and rebuilt.

Other difficulties encountered by Cliff included miners who always seemed to be in a tearing hurry, running across the lines after leaving the train instead of using the bridge, an

Porter Jack Addis at Walcot station

offence under railway bylaws. 'The railway police tried cautioning them, but it never worked for long.'

Farmers were another problem for Cliff, who reckons their sheep strayed on to the line suspiciously often. 'We felt sure that farmers were putting dead sheep on the line to be run over so they could claim compensation from the railway for a sheep that was virtually worthless!'

The passenger line at Nantybwch closed in 1958. Cliff is convinced that the loss of passenger traffic that caused the closure stemmed from a two-week strike in 1955 that forced people to find other means of travel: 'They found they could do without us when they had to, and never really came back.'

Cliff had kept in touch with his friend Ernie Brooks at Eardisley station, and it must have pleased the old man to know that Cliff was going to apply to take over as stationmaster when he retired in 1958. 'It was funny going back after ten years,' says Cliff, 'but my main reason for applying was that my father-in-law had died and my wife, who was from Eardisley, wanted to be closer to her mother. It was also a way for me to return to dear old Herefordshire. That was the great thing about the railways – they would allow you to move on compassionate grounds, as they did in this case.'

Little had changed at Eardisley in the years since Cliff had been away, other than a slight reduction in the volume of traffic, and an increase in the level of responsibility: cutbacks meant that the Eardisley stationmaster now had to look after five stations in the area: 'I had to go to one or other of these stations every day, and to all five on pay day,' says Cliff. Over the coming months he had to cope with a case of serious subsidence under the rails: 'They found the track had been placed on marshy land and tree trunks had been used to support it.' This caused a bad derailment which led to the closure of the line for three days. There was also a tragic incident when one of Cliff's porters had a few too many one night, climbed a stile, slipped, got stuck upside down and died.

Disasters only rarely disturbed the steady routine of the country stationmaster's life, however. The busy days were Wednesday, which was market day at Hereford, the main centre served by Eardisley; and Thursday, which was market day in nearby Hay-on-Wye. Even in the late 1950s country people would crowd onto the trains to take things they'd made or grown to sell in the market: 'One man used to take a six-foot-square crate of china as passenger luggage every week – he wouldn't get away with that now! I think Ernie had turned a blind eye to it for so many years that no one minded – well, until a relief stationmaster turned up and charged a large sum for the crate. After that we never saw the china man again!'

Other unusual cargo included bulls and horses, which had to be accommodated in a special wagon attached to the back of a passenger train because they were defined as 'urgent'. The daily takings were also given special treatment, and were carried in a leather bag and placed in a special travelling safe in the guard's van. The cash then went to Hereford where it was banked by the Hereford stationmaster.

At the end of 1961, following the death of his wife's mother and again keen for promotion, Cliff started to look around. Eardisley was a class three stationmaster's job, so when a vacancy arose at Walcot, near Wellington for a class two stationmaster, he applied. He was

(Left) *The Castles were the Great Western's most celebrated express passenger locos, working through almost the entire system; here 5025* Chirk Castle *awaits the signal to set off* (Milepost); (above) *thick snow at Nantybwch station – 1,000ft above sea level – in March 1958*

successful, and found himself in a sugar factory: 'The sugar-beet industry was so important in the area around Walcot that the stationmaster had an office in the British Sugar Corporation factory at nearby Allscott. I'm pretty sure that was unique in British Railways, although it made sense as we had sidings there and so much of our business depended on the factory, and on close liaison with the factory manager.'

Though Walcot was a country station it was busy because it was on the main London–Birkenhead line. Cliff was at Walcot from 1962 until 1967 and throughout that period, as the steam trains gradually disappeared, he noticed the decline in freight and passenger traffic, a decline that the railway industry seemed powerless to halt. In 1967, taking account of the new realities, some stationmasters became station managers – and, many would say, promptly lost the reputation for reliability built up over more than a century. The local stationmaster had been an important figure in the community, and it must have been hard to believe that the new station manager label, which sounded rather remote and inaccessible, would instil the same confidence.

By this time Cliff had taken a relief stationmaster's job, but it was on a temporary basis only, pending the introduction of the station manager scheme. Then from 1967 until 1970 he was a relief marshalling yard supervisor at Shrewsbury. There followed a further promotion to movement supervisor responsible for locomotive staff, guards and traffic for the whole of West Wales. By 1979 Cliff was passenger station manager at Cardiff, and here he remained until taking early retirement in 1983.

'Change is, I suppose, the thing I remember most about my forty-one years on the railway, but I'm glad I did it. Railwaymen are a great bunch to work with.'

125

Luggage on the Roof

Conductors were placed in charge of the passenger trains to Scotland; they were a class of men of a higher standing than ordinary guards: at first they were appointed to travel between London and Glasgow, but, in 1865, through a joint recommendation between Mr Croll, of the Scottish Central, Mr Ward of the Caledonian and myself, it was agreed they should travel between Euston and Perth instead.

The smartest guards were generally selected as conductors, the appointment resting alternately with the Caledonian and the London and North-Western. Mr. Preston, late station master at Carlisle, was early in his history one of these conductors.

While the ordinary guards were responsible for the proper working of the vans in their own charge, the conductor was specially responsible for the luggage going through to Scotland, and in early days had a waybill of every package.

Much of this luggage to avoid change on the journey (for the vans did not run beyond Carlisle) was roofed on the carriages and strapped down under heavy tarpaulins; the night passengers at stations like Preston, with its then very low platforms, experienced very rough thumpings of heavy packages on the carriage roofs. Luggage slides were in use for lowering the articles, and broad steps to enable the men to pass up trunks, etc, from the platform to the men attending to the roofs. Mishaps were not unfrequent owing to striking bridges through careless loading, luggage overhanging and falling off through getting out of position by oscillation while travelling, fire arose from engine sparks, and frequent annoyance was experienced through the carriage roof lamps going out, their supply of air being cut off by close packing of luggage. I had the satisfaction of seeing this roofing of luggage, a relic of old coaching days, gradually but entirely dispensed with, the manager agreeing to my recommendation to adopt the plan of a separate luggage compartment in the centre of the passenger carriages, similar in style to those I had observed in Birmingham on the North Eastern Railway stock.

George P. Neele *Railway Reminiscences*, 1904

Not Amused

In 1872 the Queen left Windsor on 14th May, accompanied by Prince Leopold and Princess Beatrice; the suite being the Marchioness of Ely, Viscount Bridport, Colonel Ponsonby, Mr. Collins, Dr. Marshall, and Mr. Sahl. A special saloon was on the train for His Royal Highness Prince Leopold, fitted up with an invalid bed. The Prince was brought into the station on a surgical couch, which was lifted from the wagonette and carried to the saloon; he was suffering from a sprain of the knee. Both at Windsor and Oxford, contrary to the usual custom, the public were admitted. The journey was not so successful as usual. Passing along the platform in the dead of night at Wigan, where usually nothing is heard or seen of the Royal travellers, I was surprised to find John Brown (the Queen's gillie and servant); and, on enquiring whether all was right, heard to my surprise 'No! The Queen says' – but this, certainly, was only John Brown's way of putting it – 'the carriage is shaking like the devil!' a startling communication, for we, closely behind, were travelling with the utmost steadiness.

John Brown's coarse phonograph had transmuted Her Majesty's gentle complaint!

George P. Neele *Railway Reminiscences*, 1904

Stephenson Cross-Examined

It is astonishing to read the chorus of wonder expressed in the present day at the mistakes, alike of scientific and unscientific men, in estimating the speed to be obtained on railways. The author of the first treatise on a railway was the first to underestimate their speed; and he was, for years, followed by nearly every writer on the subject. When Mr. Alderson was at the bar, he had to examine George Stephenson before Parliament upon this question, and here is the result:

'Of course,' (the question is put with reference to the proposed speeds) 'when a body is moving upon a road, the greater the velocity the greater the momentum that is generated?'

'Certainly,' came Stephenson's reply.

'What would be the momentum of forty tons moving at the rate of twelve miles an hour ?'

'It would be very great.'

'Have you seen a railroad that would stand that?'

'Yes.'

'Where?'

'Any railroad that would bear going four miles an hour; I mean to say that if it would bear the weight

at four miles an hour, it would bear it at twelve.'

'Taking it at four miles an hour, do you mean to say that it would not require a stronger railway to carry the same weight twelve miles an hour?'

'I will give an answer to that. Every one, I dare say, has been over ice, when skating, or seen persons go over; and they know that it would bear them at a greater velocity than it would if they went slower; when it goes quickly, the weight in a manner ceases.'

'Is not that upon the hypothesis that the railroad is perfect?' 'Yes; and I mean to make it perfect.'

But Stephenson triumphed. The barrister again put the engineer to the question.

'Do not wrought iron rails bend – take Hetton Colliery, for instance?'

'They are wrought-iron, but they are weak rails.'

'Do you not know that they bend?'

'Perhaps they may, not being made sufficiently strong.'

'And if made sufficiently strong, that will involve an additional expense?'

'It will.'

'You say the machine can go at the rate of twelve miles an hour. Suppose there is a turn upon the road, what will become of the machine?'

'It would go round the turn.'

'Would it not go straight forward?'

'No.'

'What is to be the height of the flange of the wheel?'

'One inch and a quarter.'

'Then if the rail bends to the extent of an inch and a quarter, it will go off the rail?'

'It cannot bend. I know it is so in practice.'

'Did you ever see forty tons going at the rate of twelve miles an hour?'

'No; but I have seen the engine running from eight to ten miles round a curve.'

'What was the weight moved?'

'I think little, except the engine.'

'Do you mean to tell us that no difference is to be made between those forty tons after the engine, and the engine itself?'

'It is scarce worth notice.'

'Then, though the engine might run round and follow the turn, do you mean to say that the weight after it would not pass off?'

'I have stated that I never saw such a weight move at that velocity; but I could see at Killingworth that the weight was following the engines, and it is a very sharp curve: it is a sharper curve there than I should ever recommend to be put on any railroad.'

'Have you known a stage-coach overturn, when making not a very sharp curve, when going very fast?'

'That is a different thing: it is top-heavy.'

'Will none of your wagons be top-heavy?'

'They will not.'

Anon *Good Things for Railway Readers*, 1863

My First Ride in a Railway Train when there were no roofs to the carriages.

My First Visit to London

Well, we did get to Headcorn in time, and the train came in puffing and smoking. There were about six railway coaches all open (no roofs). They were just like cattle trucks, but with seats (no cushions), all round and one seat down the centre; you could not see over the side without standing up. They were all 'smoking' carriages, and there were no notices up, not even about not expectorating on the floor, and I think I am right when I say there were no springs under the carriages (trucks).

Well, off we went and the smoke from the engine nearly smothered us. Most people coughed, but some of us who had never been in a railway train before made out we were enjoying our journey to London. It certainly was something to be remembered. The engine had a longer chimney than they have now and the chimney had to be let down when we passed under a bridge over the railway line, which was pretty often.

Then it came on to rain and most people had got a carriage umbrella, so up went those big umbrellas and down came the drips. I can, in imagination, feel them running down my back now.

Well, father and I got to London Bridge Station all right (no Charing Cross then). We stayed at an Inn in Aldersgate Street. He took me to the Tower of London, the Bank, the Royal Exchange, and through Temple Bar. I can almost hear the coachman swearing about it then, but I was sorry when it was pulled down twenty years afterwards because it impeded the traffic.

John Neeve Masters *Amusing Reminiscences of Victorian Times*, 1921

Railway Fears

A writer in the *Quarterly Review* compared the risk of travelling in a railway with that of travelling by rocket. A clerical view was that 'such things as railway roads and telegraphs are impossible and rank infidelity. There is nothing in the word of God about them, and if God had designed his intelligent creatures to travel at the frightful speed of fifteen miles an hour by steam it would have been foretold by one of His holy prophets. These are the devices of Satan to lead immortal souls to hell'. Lord Derby refused to look at the plans of the Liverpool and Manchester railway. He was 'so decidedly averse to any plan of the sort that it would be useless to lay this or any other Plan before him; he shall find himself obliged to give every possible opposition'. Mrs. Carlyle, who has been described as a fearless horse woman, thus records her experience in a train: 'I reached Liverpool after a flight (for it can be called nothing else) of thirty-four miles within an hour and a quarter. I was dreadfully frightened before the train started; it seemed to me certain I should faint; and the

 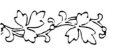
impossibility of getting the horrid thing stopt!'

Her husband in an early letter speaks of 'the whirl through the confused darkness on those steam wings, one of the strangest things I have experienced – hissing and dashing one knew not whither'. Mrs. Sherwood, author of *The Fairchild Family*, wrote, 'Can it be that these terrible Monsters will ever come into use?'

An impression of early railway travel is given by Crabb Robinson in 1833: 'On setting off there is a slight jolt arising from the chain catching each tram, but once in motion we proceeded as smoothly as possible. For a minute or two the pace is gentle, and is constantly varying. The machine produces little smoak or steam. First in order is the tall chimney, then the boiler – a barrel-like vessel – then an oblong reservoir of water, then a vehicle for coals. The expense is so great that it is considered uncertain whether the establishment will ultimately remunerate the proprietors. The most remarkable moments of the journey are those when trains meet. The rapidity is such that there is no recognising the face of a traveller. The noise on several occasions was like the whizzing of a rocket.'

Edith Morley in whose life of Crabb Robinson this account appears, remembers being told by her grandmother that, after either her own or her mother's first journey on the railway, 'the traveller was visited not only by her acquaintances but by many strangers who came to beg for a first-hand account of the experience'.

Her baby brother's bottle had been 'entrusted to the engine-driver to be kept warm on the engine'. My mother told me that, having seen a steamer before she saw a train she imagined that the train would be 'like a steamer on wheels'. There is a story of a farmer who made a legacy conditional on the recipient not travelling on the railway.

> J. W. Robertson Scott *The Day Before Yesterday*, the autobiography of the founding editor of *The Countryman* magazine, 1951

Railway Madness

It appears that so early as 1816 a project then in contemplation for making a canal from Charleroi to the mining districts of Belgium, first suggested to one Mr. Thomas Gray the superior alternative of a railway, a proposal which, it is curious to observe has since received the sanction of the Belgian government.

From this period, the idea of general railway communication took entire possession of Gray's mind and he shortly afterwards published a volume of *Observations on a General Iron Railway to supersede the necessity of Horses in all Public Vehicles*.

This publication was followed by several petitions from the author to the various ministers of state, from 1820–1823; yet, although the book went through five editions, the petitions were disregarded both by the government and the commercial and mercantile interests to which they were addressed.

Gray's first recommendation was, to make the railway experiment between Liverpool and Manchester. Yet, poor Gray's book was ridiculed, and the author pronounced to be a madman, who ought to be shut up in Bedlam!

> Anon *Good Things for Railway Readers*, 1863

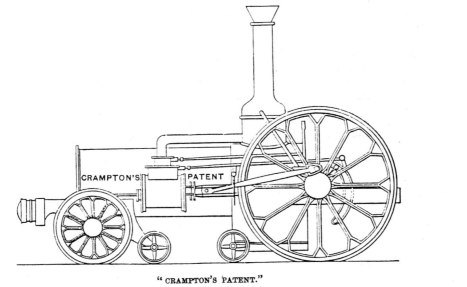

" CRAMPTON'S PATENT."

A Multitude of Lines

But there were so many lines. Gazing down upon them from a bridge at the Junction, it was as if the concentrating Companies formed a great Industrial Exhibition of the works of extraordinary ground spiders that spun iron. And then so many of the Lines went such wonderful ways, so crossing and curving among one another, that the eye lost them. And then some of them appeared to start with the fixed intention of going five hundred miles, and all of a sudden gave it up at an insignificant barrier, or turned off into a workshop. And then others, like intoxicated men, went a little way very straight, and surprisingly slued round and came back again. And then others were so chock-full of trucks of coal, others were so blocked with trucks of casks, others were so gorged with trucks of ballast, others were so set apart for wheeled objects like immense iron cotton-reels: while others were so bright and clear, and others were so delivered over to rust and ashes and idle wheelbarrows out of work, with their legs in the air (looking much like their masters on strike), that there was no beginning, middle, or end to the bewilderment.

Charles Dickens *Mugby Junction*, 1871

The Signal-Man

IN THE SIDINGS

REIN, STEAM, AND SPEED, EASTERN COUNTIES RAILWAY.

Refreshments

I believe there was no restaurant car on any railway until 1879. Meals were not at first provided for third-class travellers. They had to wait until 1893, I think it was. Second-class compartments were generally superseded by third-class accommodation in 1872, but there is still second-class on some boat expresses. The drivers of the early trains had no iron hood over their heads. As couplings were of a primitive kind, the carriages would sometimes clank together when the trains started, slowed down or stopped; the train did not move as one mass as it does today, and there was much more whistling.

Westinghouse brakes, introduced in 1870, and corridors, when they came, were much talked about. Refreshment cars received great applause. As we were far away from the Great Western, I saw once only the comfortable broad gauge, which ceased to be in 1892. It was compulsory for trains to stop at Swindon, York and Preston in order that the passengers might eat or drink.

J. W. Robertson Scott *The Day Before Yesterday*, the autobiography of the founding editor of *The Countryman* magazine, 1951

Train Robbers Meet Their Match

It is rather strange that the greatest excitement and dangers often come to the lonely signalman rather than to the busy one. Some years ago a plan was made to hold up and rob a train that was conveying boxes of gold to Southampton for shipment to America. The secret of the shipment had somehow leaked out, and half a dozen desperate characters, ex jail-birds, apparently decided that the gold had better stay in England. They therefore arranged to attack and overpower an elderly signalman at a lonely countryside place, afterwards working the signals themselves. They proposed to bring the gold train to a standstill, tie up the enginemen and the guard, and carry away the spoils in fast motor-cars. Perhaps the plan was inspired by something the criminals had seen upon the cinema screen. In America, such outrages are sometimes brought off successfully, but in England modern highwaymen seem to have little luck. The old signalman, who was to have been overpowered and captured, was taken ill with influenza and a younger man came to do the job for a time. He was a strong man, too, and something of a boxer, as the train robbers found when they came along soon after dark to overpower him. He knocked them down the steps of the signal box as fast as they came up, and the gold train ran by in safety whilst they were counting their bruises. Afterwards the police rounded up the lot of them, and they were easy enough to identify because of the marks they bore.

S. T. James *The Railwayman*, 1928

The Last Oil-lamps

Oil-lit semaphore signals lasted until the beginning of 1998 at two railway stations in Somerset. Since the stations opened in 1857 at Yeovil Pen Mill and Yeovil Junction, a railwayman topped up the twenty-four lamps with paraffin and trimmed their wicks every week. The lamps outlasted the steam era and British Railways simply because, like much of the technology from that time, they were well designed and did their job efficiently.

Julia Kehoe *The Railway*, unpublished thesis

Heating the Carriages

In one respect Scotland is distinctly in advance of England. Two of the leading companies have begun to experiment in heating their carriages by methods less primitive than the universal hot water tin.

On the Glasgow and South Western the wasted heat from the roof lamps of the carriages is the agent employed. Above the frame of the lamp is fixed a miniature wrought iron boiler connected by two small pipes to a reservoir beneath the seat. The hot water from the boiler is forced down into the reservoir whence it drives out the cooler water before it sends it up to the roof to supply its place.

The system in use on the Caledonian makes use on the other hand of the waste system of the engine – or rather so much of it as escapes from the cylinder of the Westinghouse brake pump. Iron pieces, connected between the coaches by pieces of old, worn out India rubber hose run from end to end of the train. In each compartment there is, under the seat and connected to the train pipe, a pipe four inches in diameter which serves as a radiator. This system has now been in use for some time on several of the Glasgow suburban trains and the only objection I've heard made to it is that passengers ought to have the power to shut it off when they please as the carriage often gets unpleasantly hot.

W. M. Ackworth *Scottish Railways*, 1890

Sabbath Trains

And if we are entitled to employ our servants for railway work on the Sabbath why am not I and others entitled to reap our crops, or plough our fields on that day, or why may not a manufacturer also employ his workpeople or any other work whatever be carried on? Is there any exemption for railway work or have they any privilege above any other system of labour? If once Sabbath work on the railway commences, the system will rapidly spread to every other occupation. It has been found that in our Scotch lines Sabbath trains yield no profit to the company anyway ...

Debate on the running of Sabbath Trains, 1849

No Smoking

An announcement to passengers on the London & Manchester railway, in 1831, is worth preserving. 'No smoking will be allowed in any of the First Class Carriages, even with the general assent of the Passengers present, as the annoyance would be experienced in a still greater degree by those who may occupy the same coach on the succeeding journey'.

Apropos, many railway passengers who smoke today in non-smoking carriages do not appreciate the fact that, as I once heard a railway official explain, the compliance of fellow passengers is not enough. Smoking in a carriage labelled for non-smokers is an offence against the company's or the British Railways' by-laws. In spite, however, of the increased number of railway trains in my youth, one of the things that stands out in my recollections of the time, is that, to a degree hardly realisable today, it was a quiet world, in the country as in towns and cities. No tractors in the fields or on the roads, no hooting motors, motor buses and motor cycles, and, overhead, no aeroplanes! And indoors there were neither wireless sets nor telephone calls.

J. W. Robertson Scott *The Day Before Yesterday*, the autobiography of the founding editor of *The Countryman* magazine, 1951

STEAM IN THE BLOOD

JIM McCLELLAND

*Driver on the London Midland
& Scottish Railway*

Sixty-eight-year-old Jim McClelland is saddened by the fact that when he and others like him have died there will be no one left who remembers how steam engines were driven in the days when they were designed for use, not ornament. His family may be unique, too, in that immediate members have, between them, completed 361 years of railway service; his own career lasted forty-eight years.

'My father and grandfather were railwaymen,' he says proudly, 'and my father's seven brothers were all railwaymen.' And so were Jim's wife's family; her father had the job of filling the seat warmers, tin cans of hot water placed under the seats in the days before technology made such work redundant. Despite the fact that he now lives in Carlisle, Jim is a Scot whose family memories of the railway are mostly Scottish ones: 'My father started work in 1909, working for what was then known as the Portpatrick and Wigtown Joint Railway Company; that was long before the Glasgow and South West took over, and then the LMS. The line was always known as the Old Paddy because it ran the boat train to Stranraer.'

Jim was born at Newton Stewart near Stranraer about a hundred miles north of his present home in Carlisle. He left school aged fourteen, in 1944, and despite his long family connections with the railway he got his first job in road transport. 'There were lots of jobs going and not enough people to do them, and the first one I liked the sound of was as a lorry boy; but it was an absolute dead end of a job,' he says with a smile. After that shaky start his father suggested he get a job cleaning engines at Newton Stewart.

Jim's father had been a porter signalman, and his grandfather a ganger and platelayer, whom Jim still remembers: 'Old Sam was a grand chap, a real old-timer who would have started on the railways in the 1880s, I believe. And *his* father – my great-grandfather – actually helped build the first railways. It was a family story that great-grandfather had helped build the Cree Viaduct foundations: they used sheep's wool which was apparently just the thing for creating firm foundations in boggy areas.'

On Jim's first day at Newton Stewart he already knew most of the other lads. His pay was just 38 shillings a week: 'That was for a cleaner, but it was a hell of a job, more like heavy labouring with a bit of cleaning thrown in! I remember moving these absolutely filthy coal boxes – they weighed about ten hundredweight each, and all we had to help us was a hand-crane. Dirtiest job you can imagine. You swung

Jim's father, who worked on the railways before him

134

A Wigtownshire railway engine at Garlieston around 1890 (Dumfries and Galloway Libraries, Information & Archives)

the boxes up over the loco driver to the fireman who tipped the contents into his tender.'

When Jim's career started, cleaners were not allowed any firing turns on mainline trains till they were seventeen, but they were allowed to fire on branch lines. 'I can remember the very first engine on which I fired,' says Jim. 'It was No 17375 and it was a very old engine indeed. It had a big old brass handle to put the water on. You had to be careful with the water pressure on this one, because if it got too high and there was a blow-off you then found you couldn't get the injector on. It was just a peculiarity of that old engine.'

Jim's first firing turn came about as a result of another man's misfortune: a regular fireman had been hurt and Jim was chosen to fill in for him. This was on a branch line, and he was firing for an elderly driver who clearly wasn't that impressed by his new companion: 'As luck would have it, on my very first day the flippin' injector got stuck and I remember that old driver slapped my hand and said, "I'm like a schoolteacher to you". He showed me what to do from then on. The problem with the injector was that I was trying to be too quick.'

By tradition the driver always stood on the left-hand side of the footplate and the fireman on the right, but for Jim, a right-handed fireman, this meant working in an awkward position; however, it was something he simply had to get used to. He also had to get used to the rigid demarcation within the ranks of the engine cleaning staff: 'When you were cleaning an engine there was a system to it. The senior cleaner did the tender, the next man down in terms of seniority did the boiler, and the most junior did the motions, which of course was the dirtiest job of the lot. Just after the war, when I was about sixteen, there was

Newton Stewart station (Dumfries and Galloway Libraries, Information & Archives)

a great shortage of men, and this meant that even as a junior cleaner I was working at the same level with men who'd come back from fighting and were maybe twenty-five years old. This was a situation that had never really existed before on the railway, and some men found it difficult to cope with.'

After a few months Jim was made redundant at Newton Stewart, and was posted to Stranraer where he was to remain for eight months during 1947. He then returned to Newton Stewart and worked there until 1955 when the shed finally closed; Jim moved to Carlisle where he was to remain for the rest of his career. As he explains: 'Newton Stewart was really just a sub-depot to Stranraer, although there were twenty staff – drivers, firemen, cleaners and a foreman who was a trained fitter. It was a small shed with some very old engines, whereas Stranraer was much bigger, with bigger engines to match. The engines at Newton Stewart were what were called Cale jumbos, that is, small locomotives used largely for freight and local passenger work. At Stranraer, Black 5s were used for the boat train to Glasgow and for journeys between Stranraer and Carlisle.

'I couldn't afford digs when I started work in Stranraer, so I travelled back and forth each day from my home at Newton Stewart. The lads I worked with were very helpful, and they juggled their shifts so that I was able to live at home and commute. That was what I always found about railway work, that people were always incredibly helpful. Anyway, I used to leave home at 4.30am and I wouldn't get home again until 3.30pm the following day. To be honest, but for pressure from my dad I think I'd have left, because those journeys from Newton Stewart to Stranraer on top of a long day's work were too much for me. I had no social life at all.'

Despite these sometimes shaky early years, Jim was soon firing regularly, and he was becoming aware of the special role of fireman and driver in an industry that relied entirely on skills and experience: 'A good fireman was aware that every locomotive had its own individual characteristics. Just take the variations in firebox design as an example – some locomotives had sloping fireboxes, others had long ones; the Duchess class had a very wide firebox and it was always the devil to fire it from cold.'

The cleaners at Stranraer and Newton Stewart did the fire-raising: 'We used small split sticks, just like you'd use at home on the fire, to get the thing going. At the small shed at Newton Stewart this was always a bit of a nightmare, because it always seemed to be freezing and there were no lights; you just had a lamp with a burning rag as a light, and with all the smoke, visibility was virtually nil. When the drivers arrived at twenty-past five in the morning you were expected to have got the pressure in the engines up to about 80lb. The fireman who was to go out with the driver would then spend an hour really getting the fire going and the pressure up.'

According to Jim the locomotive men were always close, and friendships that were forged in these early days, lasted a lifetime. Also the bonding seemed much stronger than it ever was in the days of diesel when, as Jim puts it, you were much more of a technician: 'On steam you were part of a team, and even today when an old driver dies round here you can be sure the cemetery will be packed to capacity because old friends from all over get to know and turn up to pay their last respects.'

Retired railwaymen in the Carlisle area also seem to be compelled to keep in regular contact. When Jim retired, six other Carlisle men retired at the same time, and the little group still meets regularly every month. And although steam trains run occasionally as specials on the main line today, the atmosphere is completely different.

'At Stranraer, Black 5s were used for the boat to train to Glasgow...'

A latter-day LMS type 1200 Class 2–6–Ts, used for cross-country work across much of their system (Milepost)

'Take coal, for example,' says Jim. 'In the old days every area had a different kind of coal, and you soon got to know where good coal was used and where bad. At Leeds we always got very good coal, but it was the sort of coal that expanded when burning so you had to be careful not to put too much on the fire. Sometimes you got another type of coal that burned well but didn't last long. Coal, like the engines that burnt it, had its own unique character.

'When I fired on the Duchesses from Glasgow the coal was so poor I was shovelling all the time – you couldn't stop for a minute, but of course every time you opened the firebox door you lost heat, so it was a bit like filling a bucket with a hole in the bottom: the faster you fill, the quicker it runs out the other end. On the Duchess class the firebox had a use-

'When I fired on the Duchesses from Glasgow the coal was so poor I was shovelling all the time…'

ful flap that came halfway up the opening, so when you opened the door only part of the fire was exposed to the air and you could shovel the coal over the top of the flap. There was definitely an art to firing, and that art varied according to the engine you were on – even drivers sometimes missed their firing days, so much so that they'd insist on taking a turn with the shovel when they no longer had to.'

By 1947, just a year or so after starting at Newton Stewart, Jim was a passed cleaner; but such was the shortage of men that he was firing virtually every day. After 365 turns he was given a pay rise; it then took four years before he got to the top fireman's rate of pay. Throughout this period he was learning new routes and going through the meticulous pro-

cedures used to ensure that a man really *did* know what he was about: 'All drivers were given a route card and asked to sign it – and woe betide you if you signed to say you knew the route and then there was an accident and it transpired that you didn't really know the route well enough. In practice that never actually happened because no one would be mad enough to say they knew a route when they didn't. If there was the least mishap there would be an enquiry and that card would be evidence.'

In other respects the system used peer pressure to make sure the men were kept up to the mark. Drivers didn't want their firemen to fail as drivers, for example, because failure was a reflection on *them*. To prevent this sort of problem arising they made sure the fireman had enough experience to get him through: 'Drivers would let you have a go when you were a fireman – I had a go at driving while I was still a fireman, though always under the supervision of an experienced man, so it was always safe. To get ahead quickly it was also a good idea to sign up for a number of routes; that way you got a lot more driving turns, and eventually, when you'd done enough turns, more money.'

Like many railwaymen, Jim was helped enormously by what were known as 'mutual improvement classes', where men who were already drivers would lecture on a variety of subjects, from the vacuum brake to the rules and the motion-work. It was up to each individual whether he attended these classes or not, and it was in their own time and entirely unpaid; but the inspectors always knew if a particular man had been attending, and you couldn't pass up the ranks without being passed by the inspector: 'He would test you on all the rules and regulations, and he was always very thorough. He took you on the footplate, asked you all about the layout, how the vacuum brake worked, how one should react in an emergency – they were all incredibly rigorous.'

And it was the inspectors who had to pass the old steam drivers on the new diesel trains, as Jim explains: 'Some of the older men were terrible when it came to learning to drive diesel – you could see the look of despair on their faces. Their lives had been so tied up with steam that they could make nothing of this new-fangled system. Some adapted, but many left. And it didn't matter that the new cabs were cleaner and more comfortable than the old footplate. It didn't matter that a steam train driver's work was very dirty work indeed.'

As a driver, Jim worked routes all over the north west – down through Cumbria and on to Leeds in the south, and up to Stranraer in the north. He also worked with many drivers, and as he recalls, drivers were nothing if not individualists: 'I remember working as a fireman with drivers who would never talk to you when the train was going in one direction, but would chat quite happily if it was going in the other direction. One old driver was particularly bad for this sort of thing; he'd never say a word on the way to Glasgow, but he'd talk you to death in the pub when we got there and stayed overnight – and then not a word again, on the return journey. But I can't remember hearing about a single instance of animosity between a driver and a fireman – you just couldn't afford *not* to get on with each other. A lot of people forget, too, that knowing a route meant more than knowing the gradients and signals and so on; you also had to know, for example, how many wagons you could get on a loop if you had to wait there for a signal.

'A lot of my work once I moved to Carlisle was between Carlisle and Glasgow; we covered this area by a number of routes, and if you didn't know a particular route you'd ask for a conductor to go with you, a system that still applies today.'

When Jim was a young man it took years to be passed for driving mainline trains, but the rewards could be substantial: 'Any routes that involved more miles than you were expected to do normally meant you were paid a mileage rate, and this meant you got extra money. London is a classic example – if you had two driving turns to London a week from Carlisle you'd earn £17, and in the 1950s that was a good bonus, a fireman's weekly wage at the time being £9 9s. As a result there was a lot of competition to get that firing, although a passed fireman couldn't drive to London anyway; you had to be a full driver.'

Learning from more experienced men was excellent training, which may explain why there were so few mishaps in the steam days. But one incident involving the Earl of Tay's engine, the *Great Marquess*, has always amused Jim: 'The earl wanted to see it before it was finally taken out of service at the end of the steam period, so it was brought up from the Severn Valley and we waited for it at a place called Long Preston. Water had to be put on it here, from a bridge, but although I kept my eyes open for the water tanker it never turned up. So we asked a policeman to get the fire brigade out to supply us – and it cost a fortune!'

Jim worked the *Mallard*, a record-breaking train, from Newcastle to Carlisle once (as the traction inspector) and remembers how shocked he was when he spotted a man lying on the tracks ahead of the train: 'We were just coming into Prudhoe when I saw him, and there was *no* way I could have stopped the train in time; but as we got near him he just casually rolled off the track, and we saw he'd been taking photographs! On another occasion we were on a Special from Skipton to Carlisle – there's a long drag there, and if you get through the second bridge on this bit you know you are going to make it. But before we got there we started to slip, so we walked in front and put sand on the line by hand before running back and jumping on again. I remember the poor old fireman wasn't quick enough and he had to jump onto the first coach! That was on the Steam Special at the end of the steam era.'

In 1960 Jim fired on the royal train to Stirling; he was carefully vetted in advance, and he can remember the secrecy with which the whole thing was conducted, including the selection of the drivers: 'They really were very careful, but then I suppose they had to be. All I can remember about firing on the royal train was how easy it was – you had the very best coal, the best engine and a completely clear route. For my one stint I got 10s and a let- ter personally addressed to me from the Queen's office thanking me for my efforts. I fired for the present Queen and Prince Philip as far as Glasgow where the trains were changed.'

By 1981 Jim was an instructor for diesel and electric engines in the training schools, and by 1986 he was a full inspector. However, like most steam-train drivers, he has always looked back with affection on those vanished days: 'Diesel,' he says, 'is as good as steam in the practical sense, but there's no sense of achievement with it. Steam didn't end, up here at Carlisle, until 1963; I was on the second last steam train to leave the station, and the last was the old boat train to Stranraer.'

Jim's last day at work on 26 March 1994 with driver David Gardner and fireman Paul Kane

Jim was involved in a very bad crash at Kilmarnock in the 1950s. He was firing for a driver who simply missed a signal, and two locomotives ended up smashed into each other and leaning dangerously over the edge of a bridge. The fireman on the other train was badly burned, but Jim escaped virtually unscathed. Nevertheless, for every bad memory Jim has a thousand happy ones, as he explains: 'My best memories are of the first time I drove to Stranraer, which is a lovely route, and of my first driving turn on a big sleeper. That was a great responsibility – I remember it was the 6222 *Queen Mary*. The first driver had picked up the train in London, but they changed crews to take it from Carlisle to Glasgow. Another great memory is of the times I drove to Newton Stewart while my dad was in the signalbox there.

'I remember, too, when one of the Cockney lads – that's what we always called the London drivers – brought a train up and stopped under the bridge here at Carlisle with all four safety valves ready to blow. The engine was full of water and the pressure mounting, and it was only a few inches from the valve to the underside of the bridge. Heaven knows what would have happened if she'd blown while she was in that position – as it was we moved her forward and out from under the bridge with seconds to spare.'

But at the heart of all Jim's memories are the demands of the engines on which he worked for so long, and the skills required to work them: 'Just take the regulations for stopping. For a big old steam engine these were very different from those that would apply to a light, modern engine – the steam engine might take a couple of miles to stop, depending on the conditions and the experience and skill of the driver, and there was no dead man's handle in those days. A modern train would probably stop in half that distance. Also, I knew of several instances where the driver keeled over and passed out, but luckily the fireman was always there to take over and bring the train to a stop.'

THE PEOPLE'S PORTER

TOM JALES

Porter on the London &
North Eastern Railway

Born in 1913 in The Perseverance pub in Islington, North London, Tom Jales started work in 1927. Despite the fact that he has lived in Hertfordshire for many years, he is still a devoted follower of Islington's Arsenal football club: in seventy-five years he has hardly ever missed a home game. His passion for football is the first thing you notice about him; that, and his passion for the railways.

His first job was as a railway messenger boy in the heart of the old City of London, and he went straight into it from school at the age of fourteen. He was sent to Bread Street for an interview that had been arranged by a neighbour who worked on the London and North Eastern Railway, as it was then known: 'A Mr Syder – I'll never forget his name – interviewed me. He was what was called the City manager. We met in a dark old room that by today's standards wouldn't look like an office at all – you have to remember this was before London was bombed, when it was still a City of tiny lanes and old houses. Far more people lived right in the heart of the City, too, in those days, because there were none of these enormous office blocks.

'Anyway, after my interview Mr Syder said there might be a chance they'd have me; he was completely non-committal, but it all sounded pretty optimistic to a lad of fourteen.' A month to the day after his interview Tom received a letter telling him to report to Farringdon Street station, and so a railway career that was to last more than fifty years began.

'The instant I arrived I was put to work,' he remembers; 'there was no messing about in those days – no induction courses and little chats. I was put straight on to the switchboard, an old mechanical thing with wires coming out like spaghetti. This was relatively early days for the telephone, and for long-distance calls a whole string of operators across the country had to be co-ordinated. I had a national board for these calls, and a board for internal calls – that is, calls within the office.

'I didn't enjoy that job much, but I stuck it for six years until I was twenty. It was just that good jobs were hard to come by in those days, and I didn't dare leave. It wasn't the nature of the work I objected to, it was the shifts. At fourteen I was doing 6am to 2pm, or 2pm to 10pm, or 10pm to 6am, and this meant that, outside work, I had no life at all, no social life that is.

'As well as dealing with calls I had to file all the invoices from the goods yard – there were thousands of them, and sorting out one batch might take from 10pm until 3am. There were few calls at night, however, so you had time for all this then.'

Horses were only beginning to disappear from London's streets at this time. Trams were still to be seen on major roads across the capital, and working people hardly dreamt of owning their own houses. When Tom married in 1938, he and his wife, like most young couples, moved into a small set of rented rooms. Then a month after his twentieth birthday he was transferred from the switchboard to Finsbury Park station, still in London, as a grade two porter.

'I stayed there for three happy years,' he remembers, 'and in those days portering was a real job. You had to be diplomatic and deal with people's luggage and with their problems. Effectively you were waiting on the passengers, because that was the tradition; now, most people carry their own cases. In those days they didn't, they expected a porter to be there to do it for them.

'I wouldn't say that most of those I dealt with were toffs, but they were well-to-do, and of course, the porter was just a servant – we were sort of invisible, I suppose. My other jobs were sweeping the platform every day, and unloading the milk – you quickly got the knack of rolling two great churns along the platform to the carts waiting outside. At first it seemed impossible. Rolling one along was difficult enough, and it would sometimes end up falling off the platform onto the line, but after a while you got the hang of it. Normally, in one delivery we'd have about a hundred churns to roll – a hell of a back-breaking job, but there were several porters, and we quite enjoyed doing it together.'

At Finsbury Park, as at most stations in those days, there were several porters and an indicator boy who operated the lights on the sign saying where each train was due to stop. If a train stopped at one particular platform a porter was needed on each side of the train because it was a single track and so passengers could get on and off on both sides: 'Once the train was due to depart, the leading or senior porter would shout over the top of the train, "Are you all right there?" If you shouted "Yes!" in reply he'd wave his flag, you'd wave yours and they'd be off.'

Tom always felt that working on the railways gave you a sense that you were doing something important: 'People on trains had somewhere they had to go, and you had to help them get there.' As each train moved off, he and the other porters would check that all the doors were closed; but once one train had gone there was little time to relax before the next arrived. As Tom explains, porters in the 1930s were kept very busy indeed: 'A lot of people think that there were long gaps between trains and we'd sit around playing cards and drinking tea – well, nothing could be further from the truth. There were trains every few minutes, and we never stopped for a moment, apart from official breaks of course.'

After three years at Finsbury Park, Tom went to King's Cross; he wanted this move largely because he knew it would give him more work helping passengers with their luggage, and that in turn meant more money because it meant the chance to earn tips. He had been applying for a transfer from Finsbury Park for months, and began to be suspicious about his lack of success:

'Basically I knew I'd get more money if I was moved, but however often I applied for my transfer nothing happened, so I began to worry that someone was blocking me. Then, quite by chance, I found out what was going on, although I only found out because one of my duties was to empty the waste-paper basket in the stationmaster's office. One morning I picked up the bin and found my latest application for transfer sitting there on the top! I was furious. Everyone was terrified of the stationmaster, but I seemed to have lost all fear that day, I was so angry. I went to see him, and I put the letter I had retrieved from the waste-paper bin in front of him. I told him that if he continued to ignore my applications I'd take the matter up with my union – and by 3pm I'd been told that I was starting at King's Cross the following Monday. That was a good example of how a powerful union could protect the ordinary individual, because without a union I'd have been prevented from transferring, perhaps indefinitely.'

Tom arrived at King's Cross in 1936 and found that rather than dealing with large numbers of people, he was suddenly swamped by parcels. 'It was a shock for me – there were tons of them, and they arrived in a never-ending stream; it took up almost all the porters' time. When I started there I did the 5.15pm–1.15am turn, which was a bit of a nuisance as it meant I had to walk home to the City. It's hard to believe today how many ordinary people lived right in the heart of the City of London then. I lived in Haberdasher Street near Old Street where it's mostly offices now – although funnily enough, one of my relatives still lives in that house today.

'Even in the 1930s I would be passed by quite a bit of horse-drawn traffic, although lorries and cars were very quickly taking over. Opposite my house was a road haulier who had

Tom hard at work checking the luggage

only horses; I remember they had one massive white one that I used to see regularly, and one of their wagons once went over my foot!'

Towards the end of the 1930s, Tom decided to move north a couple of miles from the City back to his home borough, Islington; his first memory of this period in his life is of a landlady who wouldn't let him have his papers delivered! 'Can't remember why now, but landladies could be dragons in those days!' he says with a grin.

Into the swing of things at King's Cross, he discovered the main requirement was for speed, because no sooner had one train been sorted than another was in need of attention. Mailbags were unloaded, not onto the platform side of the train, but down onto the next set of rails: 'Doing it that way meant that we could sort the mail out while the passengers were boarding,' remembers Tom.

When he started work at King's Cross, more than two hundred full-time porters were still employed at the station. Many of his fellow porters were elderly men who'd started work at the turn of the century. 'They were always very nice, if a bit old-fashioned,' says Tom, 'but they showed you the ropes, tried to be helpful and so on.'

All the porters wore what Tom thought were terrible uniforms. They were navy, with a cap, but made out of extremely rough, coarse material, and even on the hottest day of the year a porter wouldn't dare be seen without a tie and a hat. The other problem was that they very rarely seemed to fit properly, and the new man would have to go off to The Lotteries in Petticoat Lane where all railway uniforms were made, and where 'They'd sort out a new coat or trousers for you,' says Tom. Then he observed: 'In fact, the real difficulties weren't with uniforms, they were with one or two of the staff. We had an inspector, for example, who was famous for walking along shouting, "You know your duty!" – usually when we were sweeping the long platforms. Then he'd shout, "I don't want to make you do it again," but of course he often *did* make us do it again.'

Tom remembers that in his early days trains always seemed to be full: 'There were passengers everywhere, and in summer they often had half a ton of luggage, if they were going to Scotland for a few weeks for example, or grouse shooting.' Streams of porters were always unloading taxis, but if they found themselves with a spare minute they queued with the other porters at the ticket office to help passengers with heavy luggage. Aristocrats were definitely the best tippers, and particularly in August when they were off to the grouse moors. 'That always seemed to put them in a good mood,' remembers Tom.

'I particularly remember the old Duke of Windsor – King Edward who abdicated. He took the royal train often, but he'd always arrive by cab, and at night. He'd get out of the cab, call a porter and walk straight past the booking office. He always seemed to have had a few drinks, and that'd be putting it mildly! I used to take him to a sleeper so no one saw him – he always seemed concerned about that, understandably I suppose. As I helped him out of the cab he'd always say, "You know where I want to go" – and of course I knew exactly, straight into his carriage. I think I helped him across the station four or five times, but he was never accompanied by Mrs Simpson who, I suppose, preferred to stay in France. He always travelled under an assumed name, too, but we knew who he was.'

In Tom's day the royal train was always kept ready in sidings at Old Oak Common in West London, and when a member of the royal family was expected, it would be brought to King's Cross at night. 'Royal trains were definitely used a great deal more when I first arrived at King's Cross than during my last years; by then I suppose they'd started using the car more

'We had an inspector who was famous for walking
along shouting "You know your duty!" – usually when
we were sweeping the long platforms.'

often. I can remember George V using the train, we watched him pass in the distance; then of course there was the Duke of Windsor, as I've said, then came George VI the present Queen's father. All the sofas in the royal train and the other soft furnishings were a rich green colour, and it was very plush and luxurious, I can tell you.'

Tom's first stint as a porter at King's Cross lasted from 1936 until 1939. After that he worked with the shunters, which meant he helped with coupling the trains, and it was during this period that he nearly lost his life, as he explains: 'I was working at Hornsey in North London at the time and the inspector told me to leave four coaches and release the engine. The carriages each had what was called a buck-eye coupling which weighed about one hundredweight: you'd pull a chain and that would make the knuckle open, and the two carriages would then move together and lock; that was the procedure. Anyway, I was under this train setting the buck-eye when the driver was told by the inspector that it was OK to reverse the train. I only just got out in time. It would have crushed my head like an eggshell.'

When war came, most of Tom's friends disappeared into the Army, but Tom – in a reserved occupation – had to stay put. He continued with his shunting work through the first years of the war, and remembers endless troop trains: 'We always seemed to be getting them ready to take the men to the troop ships. Normally we'd put eighteen coaches behind the engine for a troop train and on one occasion we'd just formed up two trains when I heard a particular noise, one we all knew and dreaded. I looked in the direction from which it was coming, and sure enough saw a doodlebug hurtling towards me straight down the line; I heard its engine cut out, too, and that was the signal that it was about to drop. Luckily, this one just went over our heads and exploded harmlessly on the Alexandra Palace racecourse nearby. It broke every window in the train – you've never seen so much flying glass. My mate Arthur Cove, who had a terrible stutter, was thrown into an awful state by the explosion; I can recall him saying in a very agitated voice, "They've broken every fffff…" and he never got further than that!'

At the end of the war Tom went back to senior portering, but this meant an unfortunate dent in his pay packet: 'A shunter's money in those days was 55s a week, which is why from a financial point of view I wasn't that pleased to be back portering when the war ended – a senior porter was on only 50s a week.'

One of Tom's favourite jobs was winding up the indicator board, which involved cranking a big handle until the right destination appeared; however, his duties changed again in 1946 when he became a summer seat reservation inspector. 'It was a promotion, but only for the summer; a lot of jobs on the railway were done like this. You got a sort of holiday fill-in promotion which gave you a chance to move up temporarily to a job that you might or might not like. Likewise the management could see if you were going to be any good at it; if not, then you went back to your normal job at the end of the summer and no hard feelings. Basically a seat inspector puts the reservation tickets on the seats in the train – not the most fascinating work, but it did mean a pay increase.'

By 1955 Tom was a supervisor foreman in the luggage office. He thinks he was appointed because senior management wanted to avoid a repeat of an earlier incident that had been caused by the fact that two foremen had been put in charge of left luggage, but without a supervisor: 'It used to cost nine old pence, roughly, to leave your suitcase, and you were issued with a ticket. Well, two of the men had apparently been re-using old tickets and pocketing the money. They got caught because the authorities suspected something was going on and set a trap using a policewoman in civilian clothes. The two who were caught were told that they'd be let off if they said who else was involved – it was thought that it had to be more than just two. Anyway, eleven staff went to prison as a result of that little caper. After all the fuss had died down they decided to put in a supervisor, and that was me. I stayed for ten years and started on a wage of £10 8s 2d a week.

'Working in the left luggage at King's Cross was a real education, I can tell you – you wouldn't believe the things people used to leave with us. On two occasions we were left a package that contained a dead baby. I can remember the first time this happened –we'd had this suitcase for a while when my mate noticed the terrible smell coming from it. I went over and it really was appalling, a sort of sweet, decaying smell. We called the police, and by the time they arrived there were flies everywhere, but we hadn't dared touch the case. Two detectives came and took it away to the Caledonian Road police station. They phoned to tell us they'd found a baby's body inside, but then they came back with the case empty to set a trap for whoever had left it. Eventually a young woman arrived and we kept her waiting while the police were called; she was duly arrested, but later released as the baby had been stillborn.

'Apart from that there used to be thousands of umbrellas, briefcases, wallets, bags, parcels, bits of furniture: it never ceased to amaze me then, and it still does now, that so many items were never collected. Why on earth would a chap who left his briefcase one evening not bother ever to collect it when it was full of his personal effects and papers? Anyway, if the stuff wasn't collected it was eventually sold and the money went to the railway benevolent fund.'

In 1965 – and by this time the old steam trains had vanished – Tom was appointed to a carriage cleaning inspector's job. He was responsible for all the 'turn-around' trains, that is, those that were arriving but had to be got ready to go out again quickly. 'You had to clean them while they were on the platform, just dashing through with a hand broom!'

Tom was also responsible for the red carpet which was ceremoniously retrieved from a cupboard when a member of the royal family was expected: 'It was kept in a special store-room at No 11 platform,' says Tom, 'but it wasn't – and isn't – carpet at all, it's a sort of felt material. The point of it is really just to prevent any member of the royal family slipping on the platform, a genuine danger if it happened to be wet. A letter would arrive in the first instance saying that the royal train would be arriving at the station on such and such a date, so myself and two storemen would immediately traipse off to No 11 platform. We'd grab the carpet – and it weighed a fair bit, I can tell you! – load it into an old four-wheeled barrow and wheel it across the station. They used to measure precisely where the door would be when the train stopped; the royal drivers could stop within an inch of the right place, although the inspector at King's Cross would stand there right on the mark to indicate to the driver precisely when he should come to a full halt, and the carpet would always be carefully positioned so it came right opposite the door we knew they'd use.'

Tom's last job, as a divisional inspector, lasted until he retired in 1975 after a total of fifty-one years' service. He hated retiring after so long, but he still enjoys his memories and his

(Opposite)
Picture Post *photographer Bert Hardy took this wonderful shot of porters at work in the 1950s* (Hulton Deutsch)

contacts with other retired railwaymen. He particularly relishes his tales of the Duchess of Kent and certain other aristocrats: 'The duchess was a very friendly woman. Lord Lascelles, however, wasn't quite so friendly – he was always late arriving and he'd be in a tearing rush not to miss the train. He always seemed to be carrying half a ton of records, too. Once he shouted at me because he was in such a panic, and before I realised what I was doing, I shouted back! He used to swear at us too!

'I remember once the Duchess of Kent turned up with her little boy, who was rushing excitedly about all over the place; she was obviously worried about him. 'Can I go on the engine?' he kept asking her. She kept telling him no, but he was so insistent that I offered to take him. Bill the driver yanked him up on the footplate, and from then on whenever he was travelling he used to look out for me and then shout: "There's my man!" On another occasion she had both her son and daughter in her compartment. I was talking to her through the window and I could see the kids behind her. I'd obviously started to smile because she suddenly said, "What are they up to now?" Well, they were pinching all the sugar and putting it in their pockets. Kids are the same all over, aren't they?'

(Pages 154–5))
Tom would have been very familiar with the Great Northern Railway Class C12 4–4–2T tank engines; here one of the last survivors of this once-prolific suburban and branch line types heads a farewell special (Milepost)

EIGHTY YEARS
A RAILWAYMAN

HARRY HORN

Signalman on the Great Western Railway

Harry Horn was born at Holsworthy in North Devon in 1904. He started work on the Devon railway in 1919 and now, almost eighty years later, he is still working, as a volunteer, in a vocation to which he has devoted most of his life. The extraordinary length of his career can be partly attributed to sheer enthusiasm for the railways, and partly to good fortune: this is because quite apart from having lived so long, he has also been lucky in that the branch line on which he spent the last four decades of his official, paid career just happened to be a line that local enthusiasts were prepared to save and re-stock with steam locomotives when it was axed by one of Beeching's successors.

Harry's career started when horses were still used in the shunting yards and when the motor car was still relatively rare in the Devon countryside. His first job was at Starcross on the Exeter and Newton Abbot line, which still exists. He'd decided on a railway career after a lady ticket-collector friend of his father's – his father was a farmer – suggested that he might have a chance. 'Seven lads applied for that job,' he recalls,' and we were all about the same age, roughly fifteen. Jobs were hard to come by, too, and I think I only got this one because I told them that I could start mid-week, and apparently none of the others could.'

Harry's first job was as a lamp boy at Starcross. At a time when all platform illumination was by oil, this was a heavy responsibility; it was also virtually full time, as the old one-wick lamps were fairly primitive and had to be trimmed and attended to every day. Harry is particularly proud of the fact that it was a Devon railwayman who thought up an improved wick that dramatically reduced the amount of maintenance involved: 'I can't remember his name but he had so many lamps to attend to that he began to think of ways of improving them, and eventually hit on the idea of making a slightly smaller lamp than the traditional sort, and with two wicks, a feeder wick and a main wick. This kind of lamp needed attention only once every few days, so it was a big improvement. I can't tell you exactly when it was introduced, but it was some time in the 1920s.'

Harry's duties at this first post included looking after the lamphouses where the oil and paraffin was kept. After a year at Starcross he moved to the station at Exminster, although he was still doing the same job: 'I was there for a year, and then I moved again, this time to be nearer my father who had moved to Torquay and who had fallen ill. My brother and sister were still at school and so I applied for a transfer on compassionate grounds.' Harry moved to what was then known as the receiving office, at Torquay; 'This was where people enquired about parcels, tickets and reservations, and I enjoyed working there so much that I stayed until I was twenty. I think partly I liked the fact that it was so busy and the staff were so kind.'

(Above) Harry with Iris, his wife
(Opposite) *A signalman's-eye view of a passing Great Western Train* (Milepost)

From these early days until the end of the steam era, the predominant theme in Harry's eyes was the decline in staffing levels; for instance at Starcross, a small country station, there had been a wealth of full-time station staff: a goods porter, a parcels porter, two junior porters and a pier porter, who helped those passengers getting off the trains and onto the ferry that plied between Starcross station and Exmouth. In the receiving office, too, staff levels had been high, with a head clerk, Harry, and in summer, an additional clerk: 'It was very busy at Torquay in those days,' remembers Harry. 'We had holidaymakers from all over Britain and from overseas, as well as local passengers. I remember, too, the arrival of United States naval boats, when we really couldn't cope with the sailors. And we couldn't believe how determined they were to travel all over the country; local people didn't seem to have the same enthusiasm.'

In the twenties people tended to stay in their jobs; at the receiving office in Torquay the head clerk had been there for decades when Harry arrived: 'They were great stay-at-homes, it's true, but there were also some well travelled people. I remember one summer we took on a man who'd worked on the railways in Argentina, of all places; he was a curious fellow who was to reappear later in my career, though in tragic circumstances.'

By the late 1920s Harry had decided to put clerical work behind him and to try his hand at signalling. But he was a reluctant convert: 'I started as a signalman at Brixham in 1928. So many signalmen seemed to be needed all over the South West – there were lots of vacancies, but I have to admit I didn't particularly want to do it. I applied in the end solely because it was the only way I could see to get promotion. The truth is, after working in the busy office at Torquay I didn't fancy the isolation – a signalman's job is a very lonely one.'

Harry's first job was part time, but within months the divisional inspector let him know that a vacancy existed for the summer on the mainline: 'It was at Powderham Castle, a new box, and I was the first in it, though before I could take it up I had to go back to Starcross to learn all about mainline working; however, I'd already been voluntarily to classes at Exeter, so it didn't take long for the inspector to pass me.'

Working at Powderham proved hectic: there were eight items to be noted down in the signalman's book for each train, and like all signalmen, Harry had to check each train as it went past for improperly closed doors as well as for anything untoward concerning wheels and windows. Very occasionally a serious incident would develop, and Harry experienced one, the memory of which has stayed with him all his life:

'On this particular morning the 8.45 Penzance train had just passed. After it had gone by I cleared back – that means I let the box behind know that the train had gone – and I then tried to put the signals back to danger. However, I discovered that two signals, the distant and the home, wouldn't budge. I knew that the signalman in the next box and in the one behind were thinking I was only a lad, and that that was why I couldn't put the signals to danger, and they kept telling me just to try again. Well, I tried, but nothing happened, and I *knew* something was wrong. Then the telephone rang and the platform inspector at Exeter St David's told me that the driver of the 8.45 Penzance train had just reported that he'd hit a man on the line near my box. After a huge fuss a van arrived and confirmed that a man had indeed been found dead on the line – and he was lying on the wires that I'd been trying to move. The curious thing is, that the man concerned – it was thought he had committed suicide – turned out to be the chap who'd worked that summer in the receiving office in Torquay, the one who'd once worked on the Argentinian railway.'

Special trains were laid on during the strawberry season (Hulton Deutsch)

In 1929, after leaving Powderham, Harry moved to look after four lines at a place called Coagload Junction where the Westbury and Bristol lines converge before Taunton. A series of temporary posts followed, with occasional dramas to disturb an otherwise steady routine; such as the occasion a wagon taking hay across the line lost its wheel and was only just cleared in time to allow the next train to pass: 'That was a very close shave,' remembers Harry. 'I had to send six bells, the danger signal, when one of the wheels fell off the cart halfway across the line; luckily by that time farmers were starting to use tractors for some work, and this farmer had one, and managed to pull the old wagon off the line with it.'

Harry started his first full-time, permanent job at Charlton Mackrell on the main line in 1934, and stayed for twelve years: 'I became involved with the local church there,' he recalls, 'and met my wife who was related to another signalman. We were married in 1935, and lived at a place called Kenton Mandeville near Castle Cary. Then in 1946 I worked at Bishops Lydeard on the Bishops Lydeard to Minehead line. I was in lodgings for two years while I did this job, and then the station house at Stogumber became vacant. I suppose in some ways we got off quite lightly in this bit of Somerset during the war, but I remember the troop trains from Castle Cary coming along. The tracks used to be littered with the soldiers' clothes –

The Great Western 1400 Class 0–4–2 Ts were that railway's standard branch line/push-pull engines, many of which worked from junctions throughout Devon (Milepost)

---

they were so filthy and torn they just threw them out of the carriage windows.'

High in the Quantocks, Stogumber is one of the prettiest stations in England, and it is the station at which Harry still works. With his wife Iris, he moved into the house in 1948: 'There was no mains water or electricity then,' he remembers, 'and it stayed like that for twelve years! We had a deep well, and I can still remember that to fill the tank in the house we had to turn the handle of the well some six hundred times!' Electricity and mains water finally came to this remote part of Somerset in the 1960s when the future of small rural railways was already under a cloud. But business was still fairly good, and at Stogumber, as at many stations, there was even a camping coach: a railway carriage parked up in a siding and fitted out with beds and a kitchen for rent to holidaymakers. These coaches were very popular, and certainly the one at Stogumber was generally fully booked throughout the summer. Harry remembers:

'At the time I was working at Bishops Lydeard, eight miles away, even though I lived in the station house at Stogumber; but I used to do this trip pretty quickly on my motorbike. Then I transferred to Williton, which was on the same line and in the same grade because it was only four miles away. I stayed there till 1969 when steam trains finally disappeared. We'd mostly used 45 and 55 type engines there, and they did everything, shunting, goods and passenger work. We had two goods trains a day carrying mostly animal feeds and such-like, but there was also the boat special to and from Watchet. We were busy, too, with passengers, because the children went to school in Minehead and Taunton, and then there were excursion trains, too.'

The Minehead to Taunton line survived the Beeching cuts: 'It was the only branch line he left in the West Country,' says Harry with a wry smile. It was probably saved because of the popularity of Butlins holiday camp at Minehead, which clearly generated enough traffic to justify keeping the line open for passengers, if not freight; even so, it finally closed in 1971. By this time Harry and his wife had bought their house, so they stayed put and watched the railway where they'd spent their lives slowly become overgrown and derelict. 'It was a very good thing, however,' remembers Harry, 'that for some reason they never demolished the old railway buildings or ripped up the track. But it was so sad for us when we recalled how, years earlier, it had been such a thriving line with a total of ten stations, and at each one porters, lorry drivers and stationmasters.'

Things began to change when the local undertaker bought the line, which subsequently ended up in the hands of the local council. Eventually, local enthusiasts, including Harry and his wife Iris, formed the West Somerset Railway Company (WSRC) and rented the line from the council. The final act in this drama came in the early 1990s, when the council decided to sell up to the WSRC: 'I'm a shareholder, although I don't get paid,' says Harry; now wheelchair-bound, he nevertheless sits every day in the railway office, talking to visitors and checking the trains through. 'We do have paid staff, about twenty in all, but the other two hundred people involved are volunteers, like me. We got our rolling stock from a South Wales scrapyard, but it is all very similar to the rolling stock we had when I first came here. We still have a 32 class loco, known as a Collett and named after a chief engineer on the Great Western. We have two Prairie engines and two Manors.'

The now thriving line has four trains each way every day until January, when the line closes down until March. And still the line benefits from Butlins at Minehead, as well as from people touring the area and, of course, steam enthusiasts.

This is all a far cry from Harry's early days, when a signalman still tapped out his messages to other signalmen up and down the line using the old telegraph machine. Of course some inventions were never bettered, and Harry is particularly proud that the automatic train control system (ATC) was invented in the Great Western region:

'That was a marvellous innovation,' he says, 'and it's now in use everywhere on the railways. And it was such a simple idea: they installed small ramps between the rails so many yards from each distant signal; the ramps were attached to a battery, and when the distant signal up ahead was at caution, the ramp was electrified. If the train ignored the signal for whatever reason and ran over the ramp, a charge was sent up into the engine and this automatically applied the brakes. So if something terrible had happened to the driver the train would still stop before the next signal. Once ATCs appeared in the Western Region, every region wanted them – that's how good they are.'

Harry Horn at the station where he works now as a volunteer

WORKING THE SADDLEBACKS

SANDY BEGG

*Driver on the London &
North Eastern Railway*

When Sandy Begg left school at the age of thirteen, farming was the obvious job for a young man born and brought up at Kintore near Inverurie in rural Aberdeenshire. After all, Sandy's father was a farmer and in the 1930s farms were desperately short of labour, particularly as motor tractors had hardly touched this corner of Scotland; Sandy's earliest memories are of working with horses. However, his farm career lasted just two and a half years, and it ended because he knew that if he was still on the farm when he reached his sixteenth birthday he would not be able to leave at all: the war was raging, and emergency regulations had turned farm work into a reserved occupation. So he left, and put his name down for a job at the railway station at nearby Kittybrewster. Here, the Great North of Scotland railway had its rather unusual depot – unusual because it was round to accommodate the turntable that had been built in the middle of the engine sheds.

Sandy explains that when he started work at Kittybrewster it was traditional for the youngest workers to be given a job known in Scotland as a wakener: 'We had to be up first in the morning to go round and wake up all the other railway workers. My patch as a wakener was the north part of Aberdeen, and all the men we were sent to wake had to be up before 6am so of course we'd start a good bit earlier than that. It was all on foot, too, so we covered a few miles – a bicycle would have been a luxury!

'We knocked on windows rather than on the door. When we knocked and woke these fellows they'd always stick their heads out and ask about the weather. You might wake seven or eight men in a morning, and the biggest difficulty was planning your walk round because they all had to get up at different times and you couldn't get round quickly because, of course, you were on foot. I worked at this for a couple of months, and was then put on cleaning duty – and even in cleaning, seniority was everything. This meant that the last in got the worst jobs and the worst shifts; but at least I suppose you knew where you were, and you knew your turn would come if you were patient enough.

'The youngest cleaners did inside the gearing, and after a session doing that you were dirtier than the dirtiest train! The senior cleaner did the least dirty jobs. All I can remember about my earliest cleaning days is the sensation of oil trickling down the back of my neck!'

Despite the unsocial hours and the grime of these early days, Sandy stuck at it, and like so many railwaymen, he benefited from the shortage of men caused by the war in that promotion became more rapid and seniority began to seem far less important than ever before. Before this, but particularly during the depression of the 1930s, a young worker might easily have found he was cleaning for ten years. However, there was a tradition of self-improvement in Scotland – as there was in England – as Sandy explains:

'We ran what were called workers' improvement societies, and these were designed to help railwaymen know their stuff for when the time came for them to take whatever tests were necessary for promotion. Since you didn't get the chance of promotion that often, it was a good idea to be well prepared for when any opportunity *did* come along. Engine cleaners like me went to these classes so that they could become firemen, the first step up the ladder. Firemen and drivers did all the lecturing in their own free time and they were never paid, but what they did helped others enormously. Drivers also went along to keep up to date with new developments, and the classes really were excellent.'

The inspectors in Sandy's day all wore bowler hats as part of their uniform and he can still remember the grilling he received when he went to be examined for firing. He was tested on everything from the use of the injector to protecting a train that had been derailed or stopped for some other unscheduled reason. 'Protecting your train has changed out of all recognition between the steam days and now. In the old days you had to put detonators on the track for three-quarters of a mile in front and three-quarters of a mile behind.' That was the distance it was felt another train would need in order to stop easily before reaching a stalled train. With a modern express the stopping distance is about one and a half miles simply to allow for the greater speed. But as Sandy observes, walking along the track, perhaps on a dark, wet night, laying detonators was not a job for the fainthearted.

Detonators might have been crude by modern standards, but in fact Sandy can remember using them on only two occasions. In later days special clips were used instead, and as

Hot work on the footplate of a steam engine in the 1920s (Hulton Deutsch)

the train went over them the driver received a warning that there was a problem up ahead. 'A detonator was just a gunpowder charge; it was small and round and you really only got them a lot where engineers were working, and in fog near signals. If a distant signal was against you there would be one detonator; three detonators meant a danger signal. Each signalman had a sign a specified number of yards from his box, and if he could no longer see it because of fog, he telephoned for the fog signalman. All engineers might be mobilised for this work, and they all had their allocated places for when the need arose. It was the same with snow duty – this was considered an emergency, and every man was allotted a set of points to clear, because these got horribly jammed by snow. In really bad weather you might have to stand all day by a set of points.'

One of Sandy's favourite memories is of going home at the end of his first day's firing. He had enjoyed himself immensely and couldn't wait to get back on the footplate, but his enthusiasm was based on a slight misunderstanding, as he explains: 'When I got home of course I told my parents all about it, but when they asked me if I was now looking forward to being a driver I said "No" because I'd noticed that the coal shovel hadn't been out of the driver's hand for a minute all day. What I hadn't realised was that drivers really did everything for a young lad, as I was then, on his first firing turn. Still, I quickly got the hang of it, and even now I can shovel either left- or right-handed.'

Sandy started his firing career on Drummond engines, which had to be fired with one hand; the fireman's other hand was needed to hold the firebox door open. This difficulty, and others associated with the sheer arduousness of the job, ensured that there were always a few people who never really got the hang of firing: 'They could get by, but they were never much good because you needed rhythm and strength, and you had to know when to give the fire air and when not. You always knew when a fireman wasn't up to much because you'd see the driver looking at his work-sheet and then you'd hear him say "Oh, God!" or something similar when he saw who was firing for him.'

At Kittybrewster all the engines were Drummonds. These locomotives were distinctive because they had all their motionwork inside; they were therefore very much like Stephenson locos. In the south of England, by this time, more modern engines were in use, with the motionwork on the outside. The old Drummonds looked like engines from the dawn of the steam era.

'I remember how I used to get my engine ready in the mornings,' says Sandy. 'I'd set the gearing so I could oil everything without moving it. A bit of fire was always left for kindling so I'd stoke that up a bit; I'd take the ash out of the pan. I'd then get coaled up; then onto the turntable; then fully clean the smokebox and ash pan. Then the driver would bring the engine out into one of the roads. The whole thing might take a couple of hours. On the older engines you had a long shovel for starting the fires, while on more recent engines you would have drop bars which made the job easier. At Kittybrewster firemen and drivers had to do all the preparatory work; at bigger depots like St Margaret's, in Edinburgh, they employed fire droppers, men whose job it was to get the train up and ready from cold.'

At Kittybrewster Sandy worked on trains that covered the area to Elgin, Peterhead and Ballater. There was freight and passenger work, and from the ports at Peterhead and Fraserburgh tons of fish to be moved. The fishing season lasted six weeks, but with the extra work that they created, these six weeks were the busiest in the year for the railway workers.

Sandy was a passed cleaner until 1946. He then moved to St Margaret's depot in Edinburgh and became a permanent fireman. 'You were never absolutely safe as a fireman though, because if you made a mistake or were slack in your timekeeping you could be put back as a cleaner for six months as a punishment. At first I worked in Edinburgh only in the summer on a relief basis, and it was a real eye-opener after Kittybrewster because it was huge. It's gone now, but I believe it was one of the biggest railway depots in Europe – certainly it vied with Stratford in East London for the title of biggest depot in Britain.'

In Edinburgh, Sandy was dealing with freight and passenger work, but after just one week he was sent out to the docks at nearby Leith. Here a lot of the work of moving goods around the dockyard was still done by horses, and the steam engines were rather primitive with only hand brakes rather than steam brakes: 'The noise of the steam brakes would have frightened the horses,' explains Sandy. 'I knew horses were important at Leith when early on in my time there one of the drivers shouted "Whoah!" at me!'

'The old Drummonds looked like engines from the dawn of the steam era.'

Snow clearance (Scottish Records Office)

It is not often realised that well into the 1950s, LNER still had about 500 cart-horses at work in Edinburgh. They pulled unusual three-wheeled wagons that had been specifically designed to turn in restricted spaces.

'Lots of the lads on the engines had worked with these horses,' says Sandy. 'I can remember every team of horses had a tracer boy who sat on one of the horses to help encourage them up steep inclines. Most of the stuff we shifted here by horse or engine was coal, but we also dealt with what we always called the ham-and-egg boat from Denmark. And in the docks, each shunting engine had a shunter walking in front wearing a red hat; this was to warn the unwary and prevent accidents.'

The engines employed at Leith Docks were known as saddlebacks, so-called because their water tanks were built around the boiler. Coal for the saddlebacks was kept in a trailer which, unusually, was made from wood. Sandy reckons the engines and their trailers would have been almost a century old at the time he was using them, but they were ideal for the job; moreover: 'The engines I'd worked on at Kittybrewster would have been even older,' he says. 'I believe they'd been made before 1850, although of course they'd have had new boilers and other repairs over the years. One chap who was a regular at our improvement classes used to say that the only original bit of a Y9 – the engines we had at Kittybrewster – was the whistle!

'You have to remember, too, that there were no electronic controls in those days, and very few mechanical ones – you had a steam pressure gauge for the boiler and a vacuum gauge to tell you about the brakes, and that was more or less it. You watched the water level in the feed gauge, and if you lost sight of the water you were in trouble, because if you were toiling with a lack of steam the water might go down and you'd singe the boiler.'

Work at the docks was never ceasing, yet despite shifts that started at 1am and 2am Sandy stayed, until his two-year break for national service. He did this appropriately enough, in the Railway Regiment; by the time he returned, the railways had been nationalised. One of the great benefits of this major change was a new agreement with the unions to shorten the working week. Sandy was passed for driving in 1958, but almost from the day he'd started work until he became a driver he'd continued to go to the local improvement classes. 'They were really part of my social life, apart from all the other benefits,' he says.

After his national service ended in 1949, Sandy returned to St Margaret's in Edinburgh where there were over a thousand footplate staff. Yet despite these apparently large numbers the men were so busy that their engines were kept almost continually fired up, and three shifts every twenty-four hours kept drivers and firemen permanently on the go.

'Mostly we used three-cylinder K3 engines (LMS men called them Moguls), but we also had V2s and J37s with old Stephenson link gears. The J36s we used were called *Ypres* or *Mons Meg* because they'd been used in the Great War. Firing was different according to the engine you were on, because each had a different-sized firebox. For instance, older engines had very deep fireboxes because they always used cheap coal from the Lothians and you needed a lot of it to get sufficient heat. Then the engines used for the north-east runs had shallower fireboxes because they used superior coal from Yorkshire.'

According to Sandy, firemen and drivers were experts on coal and could spot the good from the bad in a second. 'I recall one old driver called Jimmy Allen, who was normally a quiet bloke, looking with disgust at a particularly dreadful batch of coal. He picked up a great big lump of it and took it to the engineer's desk, plonked it down on his desk in front of him and said, "See if that'll burn in your fire, because it won't burn in mine!"

'During the war years getting good coal was the biggest problem for the railways – when you got the odd bit of good stuff it was time to celebrate. For passenger trains and inter-city runs it was a bit different, of course, and their coal was generally much better because they had such long runs to do. Even if the train was nearly empty, passenger work was always seen as superior to freight work.'

Sandy considers that a fireman would at least have tried his hand at driving by the time he got his first real turn as a summer relief, and some firemen would have gained considerable experience if they'd been firing for a driver who enjoyed taking a turn with the shovel, as many apparently did. Other drivers, of course, never touched the shovel. Each fireman fired for different drivers, but always for the same driver in his link, except on rest days. On a short journey it didn't matter that much how good the fireman was, but his ability was crucial on a long journey, as Sandy explains:

'That's why you might see plenty of fat drivers, but you never saw a fat fireman! Apart from anything else they had to climb up the tender regularly for the water bag, and on longer hauls they operated the scoop that picked up water from a trough between the rails.

Operating the
water scoop

It was all hard, physical stuff. In the steam days there was no front view from the loco, which is why the fireman was also expected to help with keeping an eye out for signals.'

Sandy reckons that though drivers generally had little formal education, many enjoyed a reputation for intuitive brilliance, and there is no doubt that, in different circumstances, they would have been destined for much higher things: 'In those days there *was* no higher education for most people, so it was impossible. On the other hand, when I started out there were plenty of older drivers who could barely write their names, but the union representatives were very good and always helped these men.'

Sandy's first driving turn was on a K3 freight loco to Tweedmouth. 'I remember I felt ten feet tall,' he says, 'it was my proudest moment.' After that he did a lot of driving, mostly summer relief work when the regular drivers were on holiday. One of the problems with firemen working with younger drivers – those who had been promoted quickly because of the war – was that the latter were less inclined than their older colleagues to let their fireman have a go at driving. Says Sandy, 'Older drivers were so much more relaxed about the whole thing that they'd be more likely to let a young fireman drive more frequently. The other side of the coin, however, was that some firemen working with a made-up driver – that is, a driver who was covering in summer – would try to grab half the driving. This could be a problem where you had a fireman who was perhaps only a few months younger than the driver.'

Inevitably, driving was the ultimate aim of the fireman, and below him, of the cleaner; but once he'd reached the senior position on the footplate he had to take into account the traditions associated with particular jobs and particular engines: 'Mostly, drivers worked on the left side of the footplate and firemen on the right, although on some engines that was reversed. When I started firing most of the drivers I worked with had been drivers during the Great War, and very few ever left to try other jobs; they knew that if they then wanted to come back they would have lost seniority. Firemen learned the roads as they fired so there was little need for formal training.'

Sandy was probably one of the last drivers to be trusted under the old self-regulation system. On one occasion an inspector couldn't be found to check that he knew a particular road, but when Sandy said that he knew it, his word was accepted.

Fish wagons at Aberdeen (Scottish Records Office)

Steam trains continued to be used at St Margaret's in Edinburgh until 1966, but by then diesel railcars had already been used for some time for short commuter work: 'By the time I'd started to drive full time, most of the engines were British Rail Standards which no one liked – ironic, really, when you consider that they were supposed to combine the best features of all the old engines!

'In 1962 I started on what we called the Blue Trains, in Glasgow. These were electric and though they seemed so exacting then, I think it was only due to the fact that we were so unused to them. Many of us, myself included, went to school to learn how to drive the diesels and most of the old drivers became good diesel men, but those early diesels were always breaking down, unlike the older steam engines which were incredibly reliable. I did a total of forty-nine years' service and my career almost covered the entire period that the railways were nationalised. I retired just a couple of years before privatisation.'

A PILLAR OF THE COMMUNITY

ROD LOCK

*Stationmaster on the London &
North Eastern Railway*

Rod Lock spent his childhood and youth hanging around the station at Swaffham, the small Norfolk market town where he was born in 1932. He was fascinated by trains and signalling, and by the calm authority of the stationmaster.

'I knew I wanted to be a railwayman almost as soon as I knew anything,' he says now, 'so as soon as I was sixteen I went to see the stationmaster at Swaffham and I became what was called a probationary clerk for six months. This was the first step you had to take in the clerical grades.' At the end of the six months Rod got a good report and was offered a full-time job. He was responsible, under supervision, for all the clerical work, that is, invoicing, charging for passengers and freight.

Until the 1960s throughout rural England the stationmaster was given the sort of status accorded to the local vicar and the postmaster; he was seen as a pillar of village life. This was especially so in Rod's part of Norfolk where stationmasters sometimes worked in their spare time as parish clerks. The sense of public duty clings, and even today, long after retirement, Rod still has strong views about the way the railways have been organised and run over the past half century: 'East Winch, where I started all those years ago, survived the 1963 cuts – the Beeching cuts – but it ceased to exist in 1968 when the second major cuts were made. The King's Lynn to Norwich line also went then, and I think that was very silly – East Winch, a tiny little out-of-the-way station maybe, but Norwich to King's Lynn was a busy route.'

Rod remembers his first stationmaster boss with great affection, largely because he did his utmost to ensure that the youngster learned everything he needed to know to get on quickly. He was a stationmaster of the old school, who always dressed formally and carried himself with great dignity. He was also very proud of his work. 'He showed me all the little extra jobs that improved the station,' says Rod, 'like putting posters up regularly and keeping the platforms and station garden looking tidy. In those days cash prizes were often given for the best-kept station.'

East Winch was a quiet station as far as passengers were concerned, but like every other station in the land it was run according to a long-established set of rules, ones that applied in principle whatever the size of the station: 'I always remember the massive books of commercial instructions we kept in the little stationmaster's office,' says Rod. 'For example, the coaching arrangements book was like a bible, and it provided guidance on just about everything you can imagine. I don't remember referring to it that often, but you always knew that when you *did* need it, whatever your query, you would find the answer in there. And that was true even though much of the information it contained dated back half a century or more.'

Every week amendments would arrive and with solemn application Rod had to paste them into the book. 'Most of my work was to do with freight, and the book listed a number for every possible cargo, from diamonds to coal; and if a new cargo came along, that had to be allocated a new classification. The basic rule was: the higher the number the more valuable the cargo.'

East Winch station, 1936 (H.C. Casserley/Milepost))

At East Winch, much of the freight was agricultural produce, particularly grain. In Rod's day the railways carried a total of 300 million tons of freight a year; that figure is down to less than 100 million tons now. 'The local firm, which had a private siding at East Winch, was called Bull and Northcott; they didn't pay much, but day in and day out their grain was forwarded at the rate of about two or three wagonloads a day. And if you multiply that by all the thousands of tiny rural stations up and down the country doing similar levels of business, you can see why the railways could survive in small, out-of-the-way places.'

There were six steam trains each way, every day at East Winch when Rod began work there in 1948. Only one or two actually stopped, and only one or two people would get on or off when they did. 'I suppose the real trouble with East Winch was that it was some way out of the village,' says Rod. 'In the early days this didn't matter – the train was the only means of movement and people didn't mind the walk – but once the buses started going right into the village, the railways lost passengers.

'But all railway work was a matter of pride in my early days: at East Winch, just to give you an example, there was an extremely corpulent passenger guard, but he was always as smart as a sergeant major; you never saw him looking anything other than immaculate. He was a bit of a character, too; for example, when his train arrived at our little station he would step down from the brake van, stand to attention, and then in a booming voice announce: "East Winch, or any other Winch"!'

After six months at East Winch, Rod went into the booking office at Swaffham which was much bigger, although still only a small country station. Swaffham, a well preserved, largely Georgian market town, was almost entirely reliant on the railway because road connections to other parts of the country were pretty much what they'd been in Victorian times, and the train was still the fastest way to get about. It was also the best way to move parcels around. 'The parcel traffic at Swaffham was considerable,' explains Rod, 'and of course many families in the area still took the train for their annual holidays or to see relatives.'

Those were the great days of the excursion train; they were run to resorts along the west Norfolk coast at a time when private cars were still the preserve of the few, and the train was a vital means of mobility, in Norfolk as elsewhere: 'In an agricultural area like this wages were low, and people really looked forward to their trips to the sea so the excursion trains were packed. These days everyone goes by car and there's no train even to Swaffham, and I think the sense of community died a bit when cars started to be used because people became more independent.'

Rod stayed at Swaffham booking office from 1949 until 1955, with a break of two years when he was in the Air Force from 1950, while he did his national service. 'Swaffham seemed very busy to me after East Winch; the trains were always full, or so they seemed, and we had more unusual traffic. I remember in about 1953 there was a spate of flying accidents at a nearby RAF base and we had to organise coaches to take the bodies for burial.

That was a particularly poignant business, but there is something dignified about doing this sort of work with a train. More stately, I suppose, than a car. The dead airmen were always loaded into a single carriage and always accompanied by an officer.'

Much of the work at Swaffham was inevitably seasonal. In the autumn, wagons would be loaded down with Brussels sprouts; in summer it would be wagonloads of tomatoes. And there were other, more unpredictable cargoes: 'I remember the Royal Norfolk Show was held at nearby Narford Hall and we had the whole of the cavalry regiment bringing their horses by rail. The horses were terrible passengers – they banged and kicked like demented things in their boxes.'

At East Winch the stationmaster had to rely on just one porter, who did all the shunting work, two signalmen and a crossing keeper. At Swaffham by contrast there was a stationmaster, two signalmen, four goods porters, a passenger porter, a goods shunter, two station foremen, four motor drivers, a checker, two guards and two porter guards. 'The modern railway wouldn't even recognise the names of half those jobs,' says Rod, 'but there was work for them all at that time, which meant that the railway was a big employer round Swaffham. Train journeys seemed more affordable than they do now, even allowing for inflation. We didn't have many special tickets, inter-city savers or what have you, just singles and returns, cheap day returns, and half- and full-day excursions. I remember a single from Swaffham to King's Lynn, a journey of fifteen miles, cost 2s 3d in the early 1950s.'

By April 1955, aged twenty-three, Rod had been promoted to stationmaster at Walsingham, an ancient place of pilgrimage in deepest Norfolk. The bulk of the passenger traffic here consisted of pilgrims from all over the world. 'It was quite a responsible job for a relative youngster,' says Rod. 'Twenty-three was considered young for a stationmaster, but I enjoyed myself immensely. There was something peaceful and rather special about being in charge of a small rural station in those days. We always seemed to get hundreds of delightful elderly ladies getting off to visit the shrines; on the few occasions I chatted to them it was always the same story: they were touring the whole country visiting shrines and various religious centres.'

By this time Rod was earning £10 a week, a good wage for a twenty-three-year-old. He was in charge of two signalmen, a porter and a crossing keeper; almost all crossings were still manned in those days, and most crossing keepers lived in the crossing keeper's cottage which was right by the side of the railway. This had been the tradition since the earliest days of the railway.

At Walsingham the line closed at 8pm on weekdays, but rather later on Saturdays, which was the day the younger people went into Norwich for the cinema and the pubs.

'I was still living in Swaffham when I worked at Walsingham,' says Rod, 'and I used to cycle the twenty-two miles there and back, and thought nothing of it. There was no traffic at all to speak of on the roads then, so on a summer's morning it was a delightful ride, though winter wasn't quite so much fun. My first summer at Walsingham I was relief stationmaster; I was on trial, if you like, and it was a bit of an adjustment being in charge of other men. I was also tested on my knowledge of signalling, something which as stationmaster you really needed to know about. However, I'd done a signalling course by correspondence, and was very pleased to get a first-class pass.'

One of Rod's regular headaches at Walsingham was cattle and other animals on the

Rod Lock

line: 'Of course, animals are no longer a problem because Norfolk's almost all arable now, but they used to cause terrible accidents – I remember a whole flock of sheep got into a cutting once and a train ploughed through the lot; the railway workers were dreadfully upset.' He also had to deal with severe blizzards in 1958 when a number of trains were buried.

After Walsingham, Rod served as a relief stationmaster all over Norfolk. Then in 1956 he was given a full-time permanent job as stationmaster at Narborough – again, a quiet country station, but like all stations at that time, well staffed with two signalmen, a porter and three crossing keepers. Narborough was on the old King's Lynn to Norwich line, now long gone. 'It was busy in my time,' says Rod. 'I remember a big regular cargo we had to deal with was trainloads of practice bombs! They were past their expiry date and were destined to be dumped in the Irish Sea – where no doubt they are still languishing today.

'We moved masses of things: carrots to the Midlands, props cut from the trees on the West Acre estate and destined for the Midlands' mines, barrowloads of watercress for Covent Garden. You were at the centre of things, but always making sure that the station was run well and kept clean and tidy, and of course you always had to be there to offer help and advice to passengers – and anyone else, for that matter.'

Away from dealing with the public Rod was continually immersed in paperwork, for until the advent of computers, every transaction, however apparently insignificant, was noted down on paper: invoices, destinations, weights, quantities. By this time his wages had increased to the magnificent sum of £12 per week, although as a result of a curious anomaly he was paid more as a relief stationmaster than as a permanent stationmaster. This encouraged a number of stationmasters to work permanently as relief men.

In the early 1960s Rod married and began looking around for promotion. There was no chance of a higher stationmaster grade so he went into the traffic manager's research office at Cambridge. 'I used to cycle into Lynn from Narborough and get the 7.30 train. During that time I remember it always seemed to be winter – I often cycled through blizzards or heavy rain, and I had more than one tumble off my bike on that lonely road.

'My new job involved looking at ways we could get more goods traffic back on the railways – but how could we when the roads were beginning to take off and Beeching was about to axe thousands of miles of line? So the job ended up as a contribution to the closure of lines: we'd look at a line, see how much traffic was carried, and then see where cuts could be made.' Rod is keen to emphasise that the railways *were* carefully and efficiently run in the pre-Beeching era, and that there was little waste and enormous attention to detail, so much so that if a station was £1 short in its accounting there would be an investigation. The problem was simply that the railways were increasingly under-used.

By the end of 1960 Rod was working at Liverpool Street in London. He was in the traffic management office, and spent five years there dealing with signalling and the tenancy of properties owned by British Rail. It was all a far cry from East Winch. Later he worked at King's Cross, and finally at Euston where he looked after what we now have to call the infrastructure. His last years were at the British Railways Board on the planning and investment side. He completed forty years in all, and retired in 1988.

'My strongest memories are really of the early days, of the resourceful porters who would help with anything, who hated being idle and would sweep and re-sweep the platforms; there was a chap called Eric Bland at Narborough who used to bring flowers out of his own garden for the waiting rooms. I remember, too, the big old stationmaster's houses, like the one at Dunham that had no water. Churns of water were sent regularly by train! And all the old stations had oil lamps in those days and they cast a weak orange glow that was almost magical.

'The stationmaster's uniform in those days was very smart, navy serge – a sort of stiff, hard-wearing woollen material – with a waistcoat and a hat. Every two or three years we got a new issue of clothing.'

Rod has strong views about the decline of the railway, and he attributes much of it to changes in working practices. In his day, for example, one of the stationmaster's most important jobs was to go round the farms encouraging them to put their business with the railway. The decline in freight traffic had the most damaging impact on the financial viability of small country stations. 'It was a slightly mad time in many ways,' says Rod, 'because on some lines the number of passenger trains actually doubled when diesel first came; they thought the new trains would be more attractive to the public and that there would therefore be more passengers.'

Another change that Rod records with some sadness is the loss of the informality of some aspects of railway life. For instance, in the early days he would regularly go for a ride on the footplate if he knew the driver – but all that ended as diesel took hold.

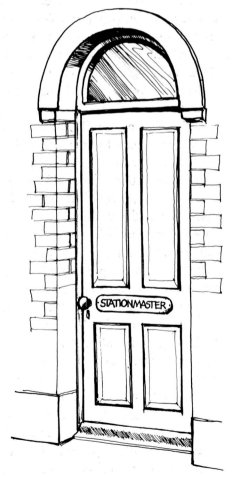

For Rod, the greatest thing about being a country stationmaster was being at the centre of the community, and being part of a meticulously run operation. Even ticket-issuing had strict procedures: 'I remember we had to fill in the old green tickets by hand using an ink pen and we used a specially supplied dipping ink for this job; it was supposed to be security ink and therefore fraud-proof. And, would you believe, every single ticket issued was logged in another great ledger – we'd put down the date, price, time and destination. When the passenger handed the ticket in at the other end it was kept and could be compared with the ledger. An amazing system when you think about it.'

One of Rod's saddest recollections is the loss of so many of the old records. These were considered worthless and uninteresting, and he can remember a room at King's Cross strewn with invoices dating back to the 1880s. This was in the 1960s before people even dreamed that such documents might be of enormous historical interest and value. But at the heart of Rod's memories lies the sense that during the days of steam, the stationmaster was a vital figure in the running of a dense, complex and highly valued transport system:

'A stationmaster's days could be routine, it is true, but sometimes the unexpected happened. What we

called the token instruments might fail, and then trains could move only with a pilotman's authority, either by written instruction or by the pilot travelling on the train, until the token instruments were restored. It was usual for the stationmaster in charge of the affected box to act as pilotman. And while we're on this subject, I have to say that the sight of a token being exchanged at speed and by hand never failed to impress me.

'I remember having a go at this one night at Narborough with the 2.40am King's Cross freight train. All I could see were two oil headlamps approaching at speed down the bank from Swaffham. Standing on the timber crossing opposite the signalbox, I held up the token with one hand while shining a lamp onto it with the other hand. The token was suddenly snatched from me by the fireman in a great rush of air and steam and noise as the train thundered by. Just before this he'd flung the incoming token onto the crossing which I subsequently found with the aid of the hand-lamp.'

(Opposite)
Passing the token (Hulton Deutsch)

INDEX

Aberdeen, 168
Abergavenny, 117
Accidents, with animals, 186
Alexandra Palace, 43, 151;
   Queen, 68
Altrincham, 64
Ambulance trains, 24
American troops, 24, 25
Amersham, 50
Ammunition trains, 20
Amsterdam, Netherlands, 32
Apprentices, 52
Argentina, 160
Aristocrats, 149
Arlsey, 82
Army, the, 34, 151
Arsenal Football Club, 146
Artisans, 58
ASLEF, union, 20, 55
Atlee, Clement, 81
Auden, W.H., 9
Automatic train control system
   (ATC), 165

Ballater, 171
Banbury, 55
Barber, Sir Anthony, 48
Barkston, 47
Barnet, 79
Basingstoke, 106ff
Battersea, London, 16, 17, 22, 27,
   57
Beeching cuts, 158, 164, 180, 186
Beeston Bank, Bedfordshire, 63
Belgium, 118, 129
Betjeman, Sir John, 9
Beverley, 24
Birmingham, 100, 126
Bishops Lydeard, 161ff
Black 5 engines, 136
Black leading, 37
Blackpool specials, 98
Blitz, the, 40
Block bells, 37, 43
Bluebell Railway, 32
Blue Trains, 178
Board of Trade, the, 73
Bombay, India, 118
Bombing, 39
Bongo engines, 56
Bounds Green, 106ff
Bournemouth, 106ff
Bowler hats, 169
Box Brownie, camera, 61
Bradford, 63

Braking, 144
Brasso, 37
Bread Street, London, 146
Breakdown crane, 70
Brick dust, 19
Brighton, 25, 27, 29, 50
British Rail, 13, 186
British Rail Standards, 178
British Railways, 13, 56, 82, 125;
   Board, 99
Brixham, 160
Brontës, the, 63
Brown, John, 126
Brunswick Building, London, 28
Brynmawr, 116ff
Butlins holiday camp, 164

Cale jumbo engines, 136
Caledonian Railway, 71, 126
Cambridge, 54, 70, 186
Camden, London, 96
Camping coach, 164
Cap badge, 22
Carlisle, 126, 134, 142
Carriage heating, 74, 82, 132
Castle Cary, 161
Caversham, 91
Chalk Farm, London, 96
Challaston, 93
Chamberlain, Neville, 16
Channel, the English, 21
Charles, HRH Prince, 101
Charlie engines, 104
Charlton Mackrell, 161
Chatham, 17, 29, 32
Chelsea Football Club, 31
Chilworth, 104
Christmas, 28
Churchill, Sir Winston, 81;
   funeral, 100
City of London, the, 17, 146ff
Cleaners, engines, 17, 18, 19, 59,
   134, 168
Clerical staff, pay, 120
Clogs, 42, 63
Coaching arrangements book, 180
Coagload Junction, Somerset, 161
Coal, quality of, 140, 174
Colchester, 16
Collett engine, 164
Colliers' trains, 121
Conscientious objector, 68;
   coupling, 151
Covent Garden, London, 186
Crewe, 97

Crews Hill, 42
Cuffley, 43
Cumbria, 142
Cunard shipping, 118

D-Day landings, 118
Delhi, India, 36
Denmark, 173
Derby, 91ff
Detonators, 80, 101, 169
Devon, 40
Dickens, Charles, 13
Diesel, 57, 58, 81, 86, 100, 141,
   143; railcars, 178
Docks, London, 118
Doncaster, 51, 52, 60ff;
   locomotive sheds, 50
Dorking Bank, Surrey, 111
Dover, 17, 21, 24, 57
Dover Sharks, 29
Drawing office, the, 53
Drummond engines, 170
Duchess class engines, 137, 140

Eardisley, 119, 122ff
East Winch, 180ff
Eastern Counties Railway, 70
Ebbw Vale, 117
Edinburgh, 70, 80
Edward VIII, coronation, 98
Egypt, 16
Electric railways, 112, 178
Elgin, 171
Elizabeth I, HRH Queen, 58, 101
Ely, 72
Enfield, 43, 79
Engine cleaning, 104
Engine grease, 71
Engineers, training, 92
Euston, 96ff, 126, 186
Excursion trains, 183
Exeter, 158
Exeter St Davids, 160
Exminster, 158
Exmouth, 160

Falmer, 50
Farringdon Street, London, 146
Feltham, 111
Finsbury Park , London, 35, 80,
   84, 146ff
Fireboxes, types of, 173
Fire raising, 137
Flying Scotsman, 63, 86
Fog, 46, 47, 107

Fowler, Sir Henry, 93
Fraserburgh, 171
Fraud, 152
Freight, 119, 182, 186, 187
French, the, 118
Funerals, 28

Gambling, 30
Ganger, 17
Gaskell, Mrs Elizabeth, 13
Gas light, 39, 78
George V, HRH King, 151
George VI, HRH King, 88
German bombers, 24, 25
Germans, 20, 99, 104
Gillingham, 30
Gilwern, 116
Girl Guide engine, 97
Gladstone, W.E., 73
Glasgow & South Western
   Railway, 132
Glasgow, 16, 70, 142, 178
Gloucester, 99
GN Atlantic engines, 52, 61
Goebbels, Joseph, 34
Goering, Hermann, 34
Golden Arrow engine, 27, 28, 57
Grantham, 63
Gravesend, 24
Great Eastern Railway, 70, 71
Great Marquess engine, 142
Great Northern Railway, 54, 71
Great Western Railway, 13, 68,
   97, 98, 164
Great North of Scotland Railway,
   168
Grouse shooting, 86, 149
Guards, 76
Guildford, 104ff

Haberdasher Street, London,
   104ff
Hadley Wood Tunnel, Herts, 34
Halifax, 63
Harlow, 32
Hatfield, 41, 78ff
Haydon's Lane, 31
Hay on Wye, 120
Health and railway travel, 70
Heath, Ted, 81
Hendrix, Jimi, 86
Hereford, 120
Hereford and Brecon line, 119
Herne Hill, 23, 56
Hertford Loop, the, 41
High Barnet, 43
Highland Railway, 71
Hitler, Adolf, 24
Holland, 118
Holloway, 34, 36, 37, 39

Holmfirth, 98
Holsworthy, 158
Home, Lord, 81
Hornsea, 43
Horse-drawn traffic, 148
Horses, 168, 171, 173, 184
Hotels, 73
Huddersfield, 98

Invitation ceremony, 98
Inverness, 70
Inverurie, 168
Ipswich, 55
Iraq, King of, 27
Islington, London, 146ff

Japanese War, the, 118
Java, 118

Kempton, 24
Kent, Duchess of, 156
Kent, Duke of, 81
Kilmarnock, 144
King Arthur class engine, 20, 32,
   59
King George VI engine, 101
King's Cross, London, 39, 47, 60ff,
   78ff, 147, 186, 187
King's Lynn, 54, 180
Kinnersley, 119
Kintore, 168
Kittybrewster, 168
Knebworth, 39

Lambeth, 16
Lamp boy, 158
Larkin, Philip, 9
Lascelles, Lord, 156

Leatherhead, 50
Left luggage, 152
Leith Docks, Edinburgh, 171
Lewes, 50
Lighting, oil, 158; carriage, 73
Lincoln, 53, 60
Liverpool, 60, 68, 129
Liverpool Street, London, 54
Llandudno Junction, 97
Llangattock, 116
London Bridge, 128
London Mail, 52
London Midland & Scottish
   Railway, 13, 51, 98, 119
London & North Eastern Railway,
   13, 36, 51, 52, 64, 68, 173
London, bombing, 17
Lotteries, the, 36, 149
Luggage, 70, 126

Marlborough College, 51
Mallard engine, 142
Manchester, 55, 63, 99, 129;
   Piccadilly, 97
Manor engine, 164
Margaret, HRH Princess, 48
Marylebone, London, 55
Maryport & Carlisle Railway, 70,
   71
Mechanical Engineers, Insitute of,
   92
Merchant Navy class engine, 19
Messenger lad, 37
Messerschmitt, 35
Mexborough, 50
Midland Railway, 71
Military training, 117
Milk delivery, 147

A work's outing to Holland for Reg Coote and his colleagues

Minehead, 164
Mirfield, 98
Mogul engines, 173
Mons Meg engine, 173
Motive Power
    Department, 96
Munich Crisis, 16
Mutual improvement
    classes, 141

NAAFI, 24
Nantybwch, 120ff
Narborough, 186
National Service, 173
National Union of
    Railwaymen, 20, 34
Newcastle on Tyne, 80,
    142
Newton Abbot, 158
Newton Stewart, 134ff
Nicknames, 22
Nine Elms, London, 29
Norfolk, Duke of, 100
North British Railway,
    71, 74
North Eastern Railway,
    71
Norwood Harriers, 21,
    22
Nottingham, 55

Old Kent Roaders, 29
Oil lamps, 39, 41, 46
Oldham, 99
Old Oak Common,
    London, 100, 149
Old Street, London, 148
Ostend, 28
Oxford, 100, 126

Pacific engine, 63, 64
Paddington, London,
    102
Palmers Green, London,
    43
Parker, L. P., 54, 64
Parliament, 126
Passenger, classes of, 73
Passimeter, 117
Pay, rates of, 27, 28, 142
Penzance, 160
Perth, 126
Peterborough, 47, 80,
    82, 86
Peterhead, 171
Petticoat Lane, London,
    149
Philip, HRH Prince, 81,
    101
Police, 122
Porters' uniforms, 148
Portsmouth, 31
Potters Bar, 34, 37, 40

Powderham Castle,
    Devon, 160
Prairie engine, 164
Prince of Wales engine,
    97
Prudhoe, 142
Pullein-Thompson, Col,
    51
Pullman, 81
Pumice, 19
Punctuality, of drivers,
    56ff

Quantocks, 164
Queen Mary engine, 144

Railway building, 73
Railway Magazine, 50
Railway Regiment, the,
    173
Railways Board, the, 50,
    60
Ramsgate, 28, 32
Ration boxes, 25
Reading, 111
Red carpet, the, 152
Redhill, 111
Refreshments, 131
Registration book, 37
Rhine, the, 118
Rhyl, 97
Rhymney Bridge, 120
Ribbentrop, Joachim
    von, 34
Rickmansworth, 50
Road books, 80
Robbery, 131
Rolls Royce, 93
Royal Air Force, 16, 34,
    183
Royal Armoured Corps,
    24
Royal Engineers, 117
Royal Navy, 34, 78
Royal Norfolk Show,
    184
Royal train, 114, 142
Running shed, 53

Sabbath, 132
Saddleback engines, 173
Salisbury, 106ff
Salt tablets, drivers', 47
Scent bottles, 82
Scottish troops, 27
Seaford, 50
Second Army, the, 118
Semaphore, 34, 131
Sharnbrook Viaduct,
    Bedford, 102
Sheffield, 55
Shift work, 20, 146
Shoreditch, 70

Shrewsbury, 125
Shunting, 151
Signalbox shelter, 39
Signalmens' breakfast,
    39, 43; shifts, 46;
    training, 41
Silver Link engine, 63
Simpson, Mrs Wallis,
    149
Skipton, 142
Smoking, 132
Snow, 81, 170
Snuffboxes, 64
Snuff-taking, 31
Somerset, 30
Southampton, 68, 131
Southern Railway, 13,
    16, 56, 111
Spender, Stephen, 9
Staffing levels, 160, 184
Stage coaches, 9, 72
Starcross, 158
Steam raiser, 98
Steam road carriages, 70
Stephenson gears, 173
Stephenson, George, 13,
    76, 126, 170
Sterling F1 engine, 51
Stewart's Lane, London,
    20, 29, 32, 56
St Margaret's,
    Edinburgh, 171
Stockton and
    Darlington Railway,
    13
Stogumber, 161ff
Stranraer, 134
Stratford, London, 54ff,
    171
Sugar beet, 125
Swaffham, 180
Swansea, Victoria
    Station, 119
Swindon, 72
Switchboard, 146

Tank trains, 120
Tay, Earl of, 142; river,
    73
Telegraph, 165; lad, 34,
    37ff
Territorial Army, the, 16
Thackeray, William, 13
Thames barge, 16
Thomas, Edward, 9
Thompson, Edward, 64
Tickets, 72, 184, 187
Time keeping, 81
Token instruments, 189
Tonbridge, 50, 56
Torquay, 158
Train lavatories, 70
Train speed, 126, 127

Trams, 146
Troop ships, 151; trains,
    161
Turner, J.M.W., 9
Tweedmouth, 177

Unemployment tax, 37
Unions, 147, 174
United States Navy, 160
United States of
    America, 131
Upton, 64

Valour engine, 63
Vauxhall, London, 28
Victoria, London, 23,
    27, 32, 56; Queen, 41,
    68, 126
Virginia Water, 111

Wagons, loose-coupled,
    111
Wakefield, 52, 63ff
Wakener, 168
Walcot, 123
Walsingham, 184
Warwickshire Regiment,
    117
Watchet, 164
Waterloo, London, 106ff
W-class engines, 22
Webb tank engine, 116
Wendover, 50
West Acre Estate,
    Norfolk, 186
West Riding, Yorkshire,
    53, 63
West Somerset Railway
    Company, 164
Westminster, London,
    16
Whitney-on-Wye, 119
Widnes, 97
Wigan, 126
Williton, 164
Wilson, Harold, 81
Windsor, 126; Duke of,
    149
Woodford, 55, 56ff
Wood Green, London,
    43, 80
Worcester, 101
Workers Imrovement
    Societies, 168
World War I, 34, 68, 92,
    118, 177
World War II, 69, 99
Wuthering Heights, 63

York, 50, 81
Yorkshire coal, 173
Ypres engine, 173